SAVING THE PLANET

A CONSERVATIVE'S GUIDE

ESSAYS AND OPINIONS TO EXPLAIN
WHY CONSERVATIVE VALUES AND
CONSERVATION AREN'T IN CONFLICT

ROBERT A. COTE

SAVING THE PLANET

A Conservative's Guide

Copyright © 2020 by Robert A. Cote

To Louise

CONTENTS

FOREWORD

by Lisa M. Grasso

The lifespan of human existence amounts to mere seconds on the geological clock. Despite this, humans have made more of a mark on the planet than any species before them which is astonishing when you consider that the earth is approximately 4.6 billion years old. We have managed to alter and imbalance our air, water, and soil systems. We are responsible for the decline of native flora and fauna, vertebrates, and invertebrates that are vital for ecosystems. Insects that cohabitate with us today have ancestors that trace back to 400 million BC, and now they are declining at rates no longer synonymous with standard extinction events. However, humans of all affiliations have both the potential and the capability of working together to find solutions that will continue to elevate standards of living globally while protecting and preserving the world around us for future generations. This is much of what Bob's book is about.

Imagine this; future geologists will study techno fossils like plastics, concrete, discarded computers and cell phones the way that current geologists study rock strata and fossils. Humans have created amazing goods and services that have improved and progressed society, but the waste we have left behind will be here for a long time to come. We must ask ourselves how we change habits moving forward in order to stop the production of wasteful materials and come up with better sustainable business models that help the environment. Bob provides us with several suggestions on how we might do this with a focus on partnerships across the political spectrum.

Bob's book was written for a few reasons. He is first trying to dispel the myth that conservatives care little for the environment. Secondly, he is inviting fellow conservatives to participate in conservation efforts. Finally, although his focus is mainly on a conservative audience, he is hopeful that people from different affiliations will consider his ideas knowing full well that in order for conservationist efforts to succeed, we must work together.

Conservatives have an unfortunate reputation for exalting profit over planet and caring little for the destruction that poor business practices leave in their wake. This isn't true. Some of the most ardent conservationists are ranchers and farmers who live in the American heartland, traditionally staunch conservative regions. Farmers and ranchers have understood that climate change and environmental degradation are real and have been apparent for some time. They have seen the impact of drought and floods on their crops and livestock. They use data to understand crop yields over time. This data has revealed diminished crop yields due to over fertilization or over ploughing. These folks understood very quickly that the way their families have done things for generations had to change. And although it was slow going, many have started to work with environmental organizations to organize efforts, pool resources, and find sustainable ways to do business that improves their bottom lines.

Looking at this from the other direction, an environmental organization that walks up to a farmer to tell him or her that the way they are doing things is wrong, and that they will help them fix it gets nowhere. Successful environmental organizations recognize that they need to listen to farmers and ranchers, understand their businesses, their concerns, and build relationships. Only when this foundation is laid can they move forward to find resolutions that benefit everyone. It takes work, but it is well worth the effort in the long run.

I am a liberal who has learned (somewhat) not to jump to conclusions about conservatives. I find that I become unnerved when I hear about development plans that focus only on economic gain and neglect environmental cost. I become concerned when I hear about friends, colleagues, environmental representatives, and even politicians who get disdainful responses when raising questions about how a project might harm habitat. I have a tendency to assume there is an uncaring Conservative behind all of it. But I must own that I don't have all sides of the story. I must recognize that I might be associating my initial reactions with past experience. And I must realize that in order to fully understand what might be going on and make a fair assessment, I have to get involved and ask clarifying questions before coming to inaccurate conclusions. Bob's book encourages us to do the same.

When we think about progress and how we might align with interests that preserve, protect, and even improve the planet, we must bring opposing sides into the discussion regardless of how much initial fear we may have. It won't be easy. It will sometimes be uncomfortable. But including several perspectives will serve three purposes. First it will expose pitfalls that may cause the effort to fail before it has begun, and find better approaches that may not have been considered otherwise. Second, it will make certain that once compromise is reached and an effort is executed, that it has support. Third, it will result in new relationships that could lead to further collaboration on the next idea. John Wooden said, "If you don't have time to do it right, when will you have time to do it over?" Take the time, invite all sides, and do it right.

Call everyone to the table. Call the conservatives and the liberals. Call the scientists and the environmentalists. Bring business-people. Bring politicians. Set ground rules like we did in school. Everyone gets a turn. Everyone has an opportunity to rebut. Everyone gets to ask questions. No name calling. Then get to work.

It is in this spirit that this book is written.

"Nature is party to all our deals and decisions, and she has more votes, a longer memory, and a sterner sense of justice than we do."

—Wendell Berry, poet and activist

"Then God said, "Let us make man in our image, after our likeness; and let them have dominion over the fish of the sea, and over the birds of the air, and over the cattle, and over all the earth, and over every creeping thing that creeps upon the earth."[1]

---

1   Genesis 1:26, The Ignatius Bible (Kindle edition)

THE BEGINNING

Remember when airplanes and restaurants had smoking sections (that is, if you're old enough)? For some reason we accepted it as fact that if the smoking section ended at row 11, we were safe in row 12. Cigarette smoke may have been wafting visibly over the booth divider at Olive Garden, but we were totally fine since we'd been shown to a non-smoking table. Essentially, we were conditioned to accept a lower concentration of smoke, not a smoke-free environment.

Pollution is the same way. Even if you live in what you believe to be a pristine region, you are affected by environmental degradation. You aren't experiencing it to the same degree as someone who is living next to an oil refinery, but you are touched by it nevertheless. And over the years, we have become conditioned to accept that certain levels of pollution are acceptable. Through lack of action, we give tacit approval to the existing levels of air and water pollution, solid waste product, and use of fossil fuels where viable alternatives are available.

I'm not blame-free in these matters. In all honesty, my record for saving the planet is spotty at best.

In eighth grade I did an Earth Day project. I worked with several classmates to refurbish industrial chemical drums into trash barrels to be placed around our part of the city. We raised the money and obtained the materials from various businesses, cleaned and painted the barrels, and placed them in public locations.

There wasn't a lot of follow-up on the project. The businesses and the city took responsibility for emptying the barrels. It never occurred to me to care about what happened to the trash after that point. But I did take a bit of pride in knowing that some of the barrels were still in use even after my graduation from college.

After the barrel project I didn't do much. I was never one to toss trash out the car window or otherwise add to the litter of the world, but on the other hand, my first car was an older, gas-guzzling hand-me-down from my parents. That ancient Plymouth Fury wagon probably achieved about fifteen miles on a gallon of gasoline and occasionally dripped motor oil. When I started college, I took possession of a slightly more economical Plymouth Valiant while the Fury went to my sister. Although the gas mileage was better and oil didn't drip, I did spend a lot of time driving alone. Up to this day as a homeowner I produce trash, use gas-powered machines, and, at one time, used herbicides to control some of the plants on my property which I regarded as weeds.

There are a lot of people like me, a lot of Americans, who know what we need to do. We know that waiting for someone else to do it is a failure on our part.

I have several reasons for writing this book.

The first is to remind people that we are one nation. We have our differences; we always have and we always will. But more importantly, we have common goals.

The second is to point out that a clean environment and sustainable practices in business, agriculture, and our private lives are not political issues. Supporting sustainable energy is not a liberal issue. In a similar way, supporting lesser government regulation and reducing bureaucratic red tape is not a conservative issue.

A third reason is to highlight a few of the areas that need action. What follows is a collection of essays, opinion pieces, and short rants built on my beliefs of what our problems actually are and what we can do as businesspeople, professionals, and technicians to preserve what we have, restore some of what we've lost, and prevent future damage to our environment.

Some of these pieces may seem dry as I discuss different sources of energy and their real costs. Some may seem controversial as I opine on taxes, the dismantling of certain governmental agencies, and our modern love affair with plastics. I researched in depth and discussed these issues with friends and colleagues. I take responsibility for my opinions and did my best to cite my sources and credit others' work when appropriate. This is not a textbook or an academic paper, so my footnotes may or may not follow the common style of manuals.

I intended this book primarily for people who, like me, consider themselves to be politically and economically conservative but are open to new ideas to solve problems. With that said, I certainly welcome all readers.

My desire is for the reader to finish this book believing that they not only can take action but has a duty to do so.

The citizens of the United States make a big deal of fighting to preserve our freedoms, but those won't matter much if the country, or the world for that matter, is a toxin-filled megalopolis.

WHAT IS A CONSERVATIVE?

Before I try to explain why and how conservatives can do their part to save the planet, let's define a conservative. Textbooks, news media, and politicians all seem to have varying definitions of a conservative. Indeed, it's difficult to pin down a definition since not all the contributing factors will fit everyone who calls themselves conservative. There are also degrees to which someone may follow what can be considered the conservative orthodoxy. To paraphrase the late Supreme Court Justice Potter Stewart: I can't define a conservative, but I know one when I see one.[2]

For purposes of discussion, I will define a conservative as a person with the following characteristics.

- Respects individual rights, especially personal property rights
- Believes in taking responsibility for one's actions
- Believes the rule of law is our nation's guiding principle
- Respects tradition

---

2   https://en.wikipedia.org/wiki/Jacobellis_v._Ohio#References

- Respects the opinions of others, even when they disagree
- Dislikes change for the sake of change
- Has a healthy disdain for taxes and a suspicion of big government, yet grudgingly admits the necessity of both
- Is leery of using legislation to force social change

I'm sure that some of my friends, both of liberal and conservative leanings, would claim my list is incomplete. I'm also sure that the liberal ones would say conservatives don't lay sole claim to certain of these characteristics. I concede that conservatives don't have a monopoly on them but, for this book's sake, we will proceed with this general description.

Following are some traits shared by reasonable people across the political spectrum.

- Read opinions and news from multiple sources
- Consider all opinions before making their own decision instead of cherry-picking what fits with their preconceived views
- Consider the source and the motives behind any given information
- Show a willingness to change their minds or at least keep an open mind
- Try to understand why an opponent or dissenter holds the opinions they do

Working with these premises, I will attempt to illustrate to my fellow conservatives that conservatism and conservation efforts to preserve and improve our environment, both in our own neighborhoods and across the globe, are not mutually exclusive concepts.

Of course, no one elected me the grand arbiter of placing people on the political spectrum. Whether you consider yourself conservative, moderate, or liberal, I won't tell you to call yourself anything different. I don't like being pigeonholed and I try not to do it to others.

The qualities listed below, in my opinion, are not attributable to a reasonable human being. If you even picked up this book, I doubt any of them apply to you. A reasonable person does not do any of the following.

- Refuse to hear others' opinions or dismiss or shout down others' opinions without giving them a chance to be heard
- Mock, threaten, insult, or otherwise disrespect anyone because they hold different beliefs
- Repeat unsubstantiated information, either online or in person

I doubt this book will hold much value to anyone who shares these three traits.

Famous conservative conservationists[3]

There is a stigma among some conservatives that any environmental concern is for the "lefties, the tree huggers, the greens…" I could go on, but I'm annoying myself. The environment isn't a political issue, or at least it shouldn't be. The politics come in when discussing how to handle the issue. A conservative conservationist is not an oxymoron. It is a stance that we must take if we don't want to be breathing pre-filtered air and paying our municipalities an outrageous

---

3   https://www.doi.gov/blog/8-presidents-who-shaped-americas-public-lands

price for each liter of clean, drinkable water delivered through the pipes in our homes.

There have been a surprising number of conservative conservationists in America's history. Some you may have studied in history class, while others' names you won't recognize. For example, there are several American presidents who are famous (or infamous) for events during their administration that overshadowed their meaningful contributions to conservation. It will be difficult to avoid the obvious as I name them.

Abraham Lincoln is, of course, known for preserving the Union, proclaiming an end to slavery in America, and meeting a tragic end. Lost in the shadows of these dramatic events was Lincoln's 1864 signing into law of a bill which set aside the Mariposa Grove and Yosemite Valley as protected land. This act cleared the way for the creation of national parks.

Teddy Roosevelt changed many things about the United States. His administration took over the construction of and completed the Panama Canal. He instituted some of the first business regulations in the world when he vowed to bust trusts, or monopolies, in industry. Roosevelt's legacy also includes the establishment of the first national parks to protect America's wilderness for the enjoyment of all.

I admit to taking a bit of license with my next selection, John F. Kennedy, considering he is the only Democrat on this list. I feel justified in calling him a conservative for his views on national defense, his initiative in the Space Race, and his push for Americans' improved self-reliance. What many people forget is that Kennedy was so influenced by Rachel Carson's *Silent Spring* that he opened the investigation into

DDT and its effects on the environment, which resulted in its subsequent ban.

From vice president to Eisenhower, to president when Americans landed on the moon, to resigning in shame after the Watergate investigation, Richard M. Nixon had a checkered career (that's a history joke). Because of all the drama associated with his administration, many people forget it was Nixon who signed into existence the Environmental Protection Agency, which ushered the federal government into a new role in environmental matters.

George H. W. Bush, whose administration dealt with both a recession and the Gulf War, also had a lasting effect on the United States' relationship with the environment. To quote *Forbes Magazine*, the Global Change Research Act of 1990, signed by Bush, "requires the Council, at least every four years, through the Committee, to submit to the President and the Congress an assessment regarding the findings of the Program and associated uncertainties, the effects of global change, and current and major long-term trends in global change."[4] This Act is of special note considering Bush's ties to the fossil fuel industry: he came to be seen as a hero to some because of his signature on some cap and trade legislation[5] that led to reasonable compromises for managing clean-up problems without bankrupting businesses and putting people out of work.[6] Bush is also responsible for signing the first cap and trade legislation into law, offering a market-based

---

4   https://www.forbes.com/sites/marshallshepherd/2018/12/01/the-surprising-climate-and-environmental-legacy-of-president-george-h-w-bush/#78b05c50589c

5   https://www.epa.gov/emissions-trading-resources/how-do-emissions-trading-programs-work

6   https://www.edf.org/blog/2018/12/04/george-h-w-bush-environmental-hero-he-exemplified-real-art-deal

incentive to change things for the better instead of forcing productive businesses into insolvency.[7]

There are enough noteworthy conservatives with a record of taking some step to help the environment to fill another book. My point is, there is no inherent conflict between supporting environmental initiatives and holding conservative political beliefs. All it takes is an open mind and a willingness to listen to people with whom you may disagree.

---

7   https://archive.epa.gov/clearskies/web/html/captrade.html;   https://www.edf.org/blog/2018/12/04/george-h-w-bush-environmental-hero-he-exemplified-real-art-deal

WHY SAVE THE PLANET?

I grew up in a part of Massachusetts that had plenty of wooded land, open space, ponds, and streams. Some of the ponds and streams were not very clean at the time because of nearby Rhode Island mills that had been operating for a hundred years, but others were available for swimming and fishing.

In the company of my brothers, sisters, and friends I used to explore the neighboring farmland that had been abandoned in the late nineteenth to early twentieth century. We would see owls, foxes, raccoons, and various species of turtles (once we knew where to look). We would regularly find flowers and native orchids that are relatively rare in the area now. On occasion we would see a hawk. I experienced nature close up and in person, not through an app.

Then—same old story—more housing and commercial development moved in over time. Ponds and swamps were filled in and replaced with man-made wetlands. Asphalt roads covered the dirt paths and some of our favorite trees became firewood. On the plus side, the ponds and streams that survived have been cleaned up due to the EPA, established in 1972.

I don't dispute the right of a landowner to profit from their property, but I do regret the loss of the opportunity for my nieces and nephews to experience the same type of childhood I had. One just has to wonder if there's a better way to manage what's there without creating economic hardship for the landowners.

In game theory, there is a parable that is often shared to exemplify the problems inherent in misuse of resources. It is called "Tragedy of the Commons" and can be likened to a more detailed version of the old adage about a straw breaking a camel's back. Imagine a situation where a town has determined that its common grazing land can sustain a set number of cows. Each local family is told how many of their cows would be allowed to graze on the public land. But some families try to place an extra cow or two there, each reasoning that one more won't be noticed and can't possibly make a difference. The tragedy occurs when too many people follow this course of action. The system collapses. It might be that the grazing plants can't grow back fast enough, or the land becomes overly contaminated by cattle waste, or the animals spend too much time too close together, facilitating the spread of disease.

In his book *Rock, Paper, Scissors: Game Theory on Everyday Life*, Len Fisher describes in detail how those who share a common resource pool need to cooperate with each other for the mutual benefit of all, else the pool is depleted or destroyed.[8]

Our planet can be regarded as a common pool of resources. Even though the globe is parsed by political divisions and

---

8   Len Fisher, Rock, Paper, Scissors: Game Theory on Everyday Life, Basic Books, 2008, pp-59-6.

further divided into property owned by private and public entities, we must realize that the actions of individuals or organizations can and do affect nearly everyone else.

Scale the concept of the Tragedy of the Commons to the entire planet. We all use a certain amount of resources in our everyday life. Some of these resources are renewable, some not, but everything comes down to individual actions. Pollution does not respect national borders or property lines.

Can we save the planet?

There are doomsayers who will tell you we are beyond hope. Others, myself included, are optimistic. As with any problem from losing extra weight to dealing with coastal erosion, it's a matter of admitting there's a problem and finding the will to do something about it.

In 1982 researchers discovered a growing hole in the Earth's ozone centered over Antarctica.[9] The initial reaction from much of the world was a massive yawn. Few people knew anything about the ozone layer, let alone its effect on the planet's ecosystem. The concept of the ozone being beneficial seemed strange to most ears, since it was often mentioned in weather reports as being problematic to summertime air pollution. So, aside from some sunburned penguins, most people didn't need see this discovery as an issue worthy of any resource expenditures.

It turns out that the ozone layer is vitally important to living beings on the planet. This very thin layer of molecules composed of three oxygen atoms absorbs most of the ultraviolet radiation the Earth receives from the sun. Imagine

---

9   http://www.theozonehole.com/askthescientist.htm

a bright summer day at the beach without this protection from ultraviolet radiation: Most people would burn within minutes without a hat and chemical sunscreen. Now, imagine that solar effect hitting every organism that is touched by the sun's rays: Most creatures on the Earth would be adversely affected, from microorganisms to blue whales.

More and more people were convinced of the breadth of the ozone problem, and so research began. Scientists and atmospheric researchers narrowed the primary culprits of ozone destruction down to manufactured chemicals, especially manufactured halocarbon refrigerants, solvents, propellants, and foam-blowing agents (chlorofluorocarbons (CFCs), HCFCs, halons), which were henceforth referred to as ozone-depleting substances (ODS).[10]

By the 1980s, the products distributed in aerosol cans and the refrigerants in building and automobile air conditioning systems and refrigerators were part of everyday life. Debate started on what to do about these harmful practices; there was even discussion of banning aerosols and air conditioning.

Of course, the bans didn't happen. What happened instead was that many aerosol cans were charged with a less harmful gas such as nitrogen or carbon dioxide (more on this later). A safer yet still effective refrigerant was also developed for new refrigerators and air conditioning systems.

Another change was in the way existing cooling appliances were serviced. There was a time when your friendly neighborhood auto shop or home appliance repairman, upon servicing home or auto cooling or refrigerating equipment, would allow any refrigerant in a system to simply bleed out into the air before replacing parts. This was not directly dangerous

---

10	https://en.wikipedia.org/wiki/Ozone_depletion

to animal life since at the ground level the gas, commonly called Freon, was essentially inert. It was only when it came into contact with ozone that it caused a problem. Thus, new processes and equipment were developed to greatly reduce the amount of Freon released. Today, responsible service technicians attach a refrigerant recovery tool that removes Freon from the system. After repairs, the refrigerant can be reused.

There were other factors involved in attempts to reduce the ozone deficit in the atmosphere. The result is that the hole over Antarctica was recently measured at its smallest in decades. With cooperation from industry and public demand and some help from the Environmental Protection Agency and its counterparts in other nations, the hole in the ozone layer is shrinking.[11]

My summation presents a rosy history of the events. The process of phasing out ozone-destroying chemicals was not easy; there was controversy over whether or not it was a problem, as well as over the severity of the problem. Industries claimed they would be bankrupted. People were told (wrongfully) that cool cars and cold beer would be a thing of the past. But the result was, for lack of a better term, cooperation between political will, industrial ingenuity, and a bit of a regulatory kick from the world's governments.

Let's examine a success story on a smaller and more terrestrial scale: the case of the Blackstone River that runs from Worcester, Massachusetts to Pawtucket, Rhode Island.

Historians credit the power of the Blackstone River as a major catalyst in the American Industrial Revolution since Samuel Slater built his first textile mill along its banks in

---

11   https://www.noaa.gov/news/2019-ozone-hole-is-smallest-ever-recorded

Pawtucket Rhode Island. At first the use of the Blackstone's water was benign. Simple water wheels provided power to the textile looms and spindles. Eventually, things got toxic. As population centers grew and formed cities and towns around such mills, municipalities along the Blackstone began using it as an outlet for sewerage systems. In addition, the mills began dumping water polluted with the chemicals they used to dye and condition cloth and machinery lubricants.

As the industrial base in the Blackstone Valley corridor diversified into machine shops and chemical plants in the late nineteenth to mid-twentieth century, the Blackstone became a mostly dead, open sewer which dumped toxins into Narragansett Bay. People were warned to stay away from the river. Bird and wildlife sightings along its banks became very rare. I never heard anyone mention seeing a turtle sunning itself on a rock along the river.

Early in the Industrial Revolution, the Blackstone and subsequently Narragansett Bay could handle some of the discharge—but over time, too many people contributed to the pollution. These bodies of water eventually could no longer handle the abuse.

To add further insult, the marshlands in the lower part of the Blackstone Valley in Lincoln and Cumberland, Rhode Island were drained and paved over for parking lots and a drive-in movie theater. These marshlands, which had been essential to helping filter pollutants before the river drained into the bay, were viewed as a waste of space.

By the mid-1970s some people regarded what was once the economic engine of central Massachusetts and eastern Rhode Island as irredeemable. Fortunately, "some" did not mean the majority.

The Blackstone River was saved through a number of factors, among these the formation of the Environmental Protection Agency and the cooperation of the governments of Massachusetts, Rhode Island, and the cities and towns that lined the river.

- Regulations and standards were put into place to qualify what chemicals could be dumped into the river and at what levels. Solvents, paints, and dyes had to be captured and disposed of in a responsible manner.
- The municipalities in the watershed built or upgraded their existing sanitary sewer systems so that only treated water would flow into the river. Homes in the area that once had private sanitary systems were tied into municipal systems.
- Trash that had been dumped into the river was removed (an ongoing effort) including junk cars, used tires, discarded household appliances, and myriad other items that don't belong in a river.

In the 1980s the Lonsdale Drive-in Theater in the Lonsdale sections of Lincoln and Cumberland, Rhode Island permanently closed, and the property remained abandoned for years. But once again with cooperation from state, federal, and local governments, some grant money, and the work of local businesses, the remains of the drive-in theater were removed, the pavement was ripped out, and the marshlands were recreated. This happened at the same time as a recreational trail from Valley Falls, Rhode Island to (eventually) Worcester, Massachusetts was being designed. The trail follows the river, some canals, and the Providence & Worcester Railroad tracks, and it runs right along the restored marshlands. Wildlife sightings of deer, foxes, and turtles of various species are now frequent. If you are there early in the morning or late afternoon into early evening, different types of frogs can be heard in the wetlands. People even fish in the river.

As I said, this success story was the result of many parties' cooperation and wasn't accomplished without a lot of debate and conflict—but it was accomplished. I give due credit to government agencies and businesses, but entities like these are not autonomous machines. They are comprised of people. People of many different backgrounds and interests came together for a common goal.

For those who question whether it was worth the expense and effort, the answer is yes. One of the biggest industries in Rhode Island is tourism. The Blackstone Valley Bikeway is part of a network of paths and marked roadways in Rhode Island that will one day be part of a New England-wide system of recreational trails. This network of trails has become an integral part of the natural and man-made draws that bring tourists to Rhode Island. I myself am a regular user of the path. If you have the stamina, you can ride a bicycle from Woonsocket to the beaches in Bristol while spending a minimum number of miles sharing roads with motor vehicles.

Whether it be a global issue like a hole in the ozone or a regional one like reclaiming a river, there aren't many problems that can't be solved through cooperation.

GIBB'S RULE #45

For years the CBS television network has run a dramatic series called *NCIS*. The main character is an investigator for the Naval Criminal Investigative Service named Leroy Jethro Gibbs, played by actor and former college football player Mark Harmon. Like many successful television characters, Jethro Gibbs is quirky. One of his quirks is the set of firm rules by which he leads his personal and professional lives. Rule 45 is "Clean up your mess." Its meaning is obvious: Take responsibility for your actions and, if you do something wrong, the only one to make it right is you.

Many of the innumerable messes in this world were created either by entities that no longer exist or because of a lack of specificity in legislation which may not make the culprits legally responsible for cleaning their messes up. Okay, maybe we didn't create the messes in this world, and we have no legal responsibility for mitigating them. But that grade-school attitude of, "I didn't make the mess, let someone else clean it up," isn't going to make the world any better.

Going back to the example of the Blackstone River and in an attempt to maintain a positive attitude in this book, we can assume that the factory owners and city officials who allowed the Blackstone River to become polluted in the first place were not necessarily evil or corrupt. I don't believe their intention was destroy the regional ecosystem or ruin the river for future generations. Theirs was simple ignorance of the consequences.

The assumption of the nineteenth century was that the waters could handle what was poured into them. By the time the early twentieth century rolled around, people began to realize that the sewage and industrial chemicals were very bad for people, plants, and animals but didn't have the political power or the will to stop it. As I was growing up, there seemed to be a widespread sense of resignation. People realized what had been done, but the companies and municipalities that continued to pollute complained that if they stopped the pollution, then they would go bankrupt. This was heard mostly from the companies claiming that if they were forced to dispose of their waste products in any other manner than dumping them, they would go out of business and the regional economy would be ruined. Eventually a large number of parties in the region were forced to clean up the mess, as I said earlier. But it worked. The area became much more livable.

Most of us have experience in cleaning up other people's messes. Many people live in communities where annual removal of trash and garbage from open land, rivers, and ponds take place. These are normally conducted on weekends around April 22, also known as Earth Day. Perhaps you have personally participated in such an event. When hard at work, most people aren't thinking of the motives of the people who dumped the trash, thus making it someone else's problem;

they are focused on getting it out of the environment and finding a responsible way to dispose of it. The next morning, while nursing aches and bruises as a result of the manual labor—then we might start cursing the people who dumped that trash in the first place.

It should be noted that many of the offending companies in the Blackstone case have since closed up shop or moved. This was not a result of the changing regulations but rather a factor of the changing economy. The Blackstone Valley corridor is now known for its technical and financial services companies. The city of Worcester has also greatly expanded one of its alternative industries: education. There are more colleges and universities in Worcester, Massachusetts than any other New England city besides Boston. An interesting note is that many of the former mill and factory buildings that still stand along the river have been converted to other uses such as housing.

Other environmental issues were caused by ignorance rather than indifference. The parties involved did not consider the full consequences of what they were doing or did not expect that the consequences would be serious. The economic benefit seemed to outweigh the potential for damage.

Allow me to go off on a bit of a tangent. Over the years, weapons have been developed which their creators naively assumed would make war so horrible that their use would be unthinkable, and therefore nations would be forced to find more peaceful ways to settle their disputes. For example, Richard Gatling and Alfred Nobel both envisioned their inventions as deterrents to conflict. The developers of the atomic weapons even thought that their inventions would have peaceful uses, such as massive construction projects, weather control, and even powering interplanetary travel. Gatling and Nobel underestimated the ability of humans to become inured with the horror of warfare. Also, they did not understand the full effects of the radiation and fallout that would be produced by nuclear bombs.[12]

The point of this digression is that even with the best of intent, there were serious negative consequences to the actions of the men involved (side note, it was mostly men at the time).

The first people to discover that coal could be used for a fire that would last longer, burn hotter, and eventually cost less than a wood-fueled fire did not use coal with the intention of producing toxic clouds of smog over New York, Pittsburg, and London and later over New Delhi and Beijing. Unfortunately, however, that was the result. For some countries, these toxic clouds are still a problem.

The issues of pollution in its many forms and ruminations on what the conservative in all of us can do about them will be addressed in subsequent chapters. Some of the actions you can take are on a personal level, while some will require a degree of cooperation with others. Try to keep the mood positive. You may not always agree with others who lie elsewhere on the political spectrum on specific methods of fixing the world, but you can agree on what the goals are. The hard work will be getting together with others and debating

---

12   Fortunately for human beings and other Earth-bound carbon-based life forms, the problem with nuclear weapon radiation was discovered before any non-test detonations. Atmospheric, exo-atmospheric, and underwater testing of nuclear weapons was banned by the United States and the Soviet Union by the Partial Test Ban Treaty of 1963. Most of the world's nuclear powers have also signed the agreement. China, France, and North Korea are three notable non-signatories to the treaty. These countries have abided by the agreement even though they did not ratify it. Visit: https://2009-2017.state.gov/t/isn/4797.htm

the course of action. Will you question each other's motives? Sure, you may have valid suspicions of what another person has to gain from fighting for a beach to become free of crude oil, for a lake to become swimmable, or for somebody to be able to go outside for a breath of fresh air. Regardless of what another party may gain from those things, you win too.

THE ETERNAL POLLUTANT?

Quiz time. According to the American Film Institute, what is the forty-second most popular line from an American-made movie? Hint: It's one word and it was spoken to a young Dustin Hoffman by renowned character actor Walter Brooke in the movie "The Graduate."[13] Do I have to tell you? Okay, the line is, "Plastics."

For those who are not classic movie fans, the context of the conversation is a party thrown in honor of the recent college graduate played by Hoffman. Brooke's character is trying to give some career advice.

The movie came out in 1967 and was based on a 1963 novel of the same name. This was a time when plastic was coming into its own. When the novel was written, plastic was not nearly as prevalent as it is sixty years later. Single-use items like coffee cups, disposable plates, and coffee stirrers were usually made from paper or wood.

To say that plastic is ubiquitous would almost seem to be an understatement if it weren't for the fact that ubiquitous

---

13   https://www.afi.com/afis-100-years-100-movie-quotes/

literally means "everywhere." If you are under forty years old, then it is possible that you have never been in a room that does not contain plastic in some form (historical sites being the possible exception). I'm not just referring to the credit cards in your wallet.

The first thing you touched this morning was probably the plastic snooze button on your alarm clock or the plastic case of your cell phone when you shut off the alarm and then checked for any overnight messages. The last thing I touch in the evening is my set of plastic-framed reading glasses as I place them on the nightstand. (My wife usually turns off the light with its plastic switch.) Thousands of bicyclists, skateboarders, and skiers of all ages have avoided serious brain injuries because they wear plastic hard-shelled helmets with plastic foam lining.

Plastic actually had its start in the early part of the twentieth century when a Swiss chemist found a way to combine phenol and formaldehyde into a moldable, strong, non-conductive, heat-resistant material. The material, formally known as polyoxybenzylmethylenglycolanhydride[14] was dubbed Bakelite.

The timing of the development of Bakelite coincided nicely with the growth of the still new electronics industry. Before Bakelite, manufacturers of telephones and telegraphs relied on minerals, glass, ceramic, wood, rubber, and other non-conductive materials as insulators and cabinets. Bakelite could be molded and used as a substitute.

Over the century, Bakelite was used in innumerable applications from telephones to the control knobs on airplanes. Table radios from the 1950s and 1960s made with Bakelite cases are considered collectors' items.

---

14   https://en.wikipedia.org/wiki/Bakelite

Shortly after World War II more of the plastics that we are familiar with today were developed. They slowly made their way into manufacturing of some toys and household items. Prior to the release of the movie "The Graduate" many children's toys were made of metal, cloth, wood, or cardboard. But plastic was making its way into the business. Around the time of "The Graduate," plastic toys were on the rise.

At that point, most of the items produced with plastic were meant to be permanent or at least have a long life. Plastic came in very handy for lighter-weight cars, more durable telephones, and more. Until the 1970s single-use plastics were relatively rare. True, disposable utensils were available since the '40s, but their use didn't really take off until the increase in the popularity of takeout food.[15] Fast food helped increase the use of single-use plastics such as paper drinking straws. McDonalds started to use plastic for other purposes: They served in plastic foam containers out of concern that the paper alternative would destroy too many trees. The use of foam expanded to other products. Paper takeout coffee cups all but disappeared.

Single-use plastics continued to increase as we marched toward the new millennium. Paper bags all but disappeared from department and grocery stores. The question "Paper or plastic?" in reference to bagging options disappeared, only to become a tired joke about the rise of our various payment options.

Arguments for the use of foam and plastic bags over paper alternatives sprang up. They seem almost cynical now; the most common was that trees were being saved and the tonnage of plastic was less than the tonnage for other waste

---

15   https://www.nationalgeographic.com/environment/2019/06/carrying-your-own-fork-spoon-help-plastic-crisis/

if paper or cardboard were used. This is true. A cubic yard of plastic waste weighs less than a cubic yard of cardboard. The arguments favoring plastic never mention the factor of volume, however.[16] Moreover, advocates for single-use plastic products—and yes, they do exist—leave out one of the most pernicious trait of plastic: it lasts nearly forever. Whereas food or paper may take years or decades to break down, most plastics will take centuries.

Plastics won't go away

People have different reactions when confronted with bad news, especially when a disturbing graphic accompanies it. Some people are shocked into taking action, some are shocked and confused into doing nothing, and some deny what they are seeing.

Let's talk about a photograph that circulated in the news and social media a few years back. A sea turtle is shown with a plastic drinking straw jammed into a nostril. Fortunately, after the photo was taken, rescuers were able to remove the straw and release the turtle, presumably before any permanent damage was done.

For some, this image was a call to action. These people quit using plastic drinking straws. A few even called for an international ban on drinking straws. And for others, a proposed ban is unneeded and frivolous; they asked sarcastically how banning straws was going to save the planet. Those scoffers were missing the point. The problem is not just plastic drinking straws, but all improperly disposed of plastic

---

16   https://www.epa.gov/facts-and-figures-about-materials-waste-and-recycling/national-overview-facts-and-figures-materials

that is harming the environment. The straw in the turtle's nose provided a tangible example of the direct harm dumped plastic can cause.

Closer to home—at least, to my home—is another example of the blight that improperly disposed of plastic brings to the environment. I wonder whether people simply aren't bothered by plastic waste littered about or they have become inured to the sight, like how we don't notice that old spot on the kitchen wall after a while. Or maybe I just spend a lot of time using slower methods of transportation such as a bicycle or kayak, which gives me the chance to notice the trash. Even on a short bike ride along the local recreation paths or nearby country roads, I will notice (mostly) plastic trash along my route more often than not. Foam cups, plastic bags, and plastic fifty-milliliter liquor bottles are the most common. The Fireball whiskey bottles with their cheerful red caps really stand out. Carelessly discarded plastic bags caught in tree branches and shrubs are especially noticeable in the late fall and spring before leaves have formed. Once the leaves are out and ground cover grows along the sides of the road, the trash is less noticeable to people driving by at fifty miles per hour.

Plastic bags are especially prevalent around shopping areas. There is a nearby upscale retail outlet center (how's that for an ironic number of contradictions in one sentence?) that boasts a very well-kept parking lot and common areas. Running alongside this complex and following some train tracks is an unofficial bicycle path. From this path you can see the area surrounding the complex is virtually draped in plastic bags and similar debris, much of which was left behind by ignorant or careless shoppers.

A few miles to the south of the outlet stores are a couple of small lakes (or large ponds, depending on your perspective) that are perfect for some easy kayaking. Plastic debris lands in water just as it gets caught in trees. Yes, paper also gets blown into the water, but that eventually breaks down. These ponds are drained by small streams that eventually lead into a watershed that empties into Narragansett Bay. With the water flows plastic into the bay and from there into the Atlantic Ocean, where it joins the existing masses of floating plastic. Everyone has heard reports of the colossal amount of plastic forming floating islands in the ocean.[17] Marine animals, mistaking plastic for food, are paying dearly with injuries and death.[18]

Blights on the scenery and marine animal injuries aside, there is a facet of plastic pollution that is even more insidious. The structure of one-use plastic items will, over centuries, break down. However, just because the plastic from bags and containers seems to disappear or take on an unrecognizable form in a few years doesn't mean it's gone. Plastic objects will fall apart eventually and break apart into smaller pieces, but even then, plastic does not decompose to its elemental level but lasts even longer in the form of microplastics. Microplastics are microscopic particles of plastic molecules that are still in the environment. Microplastic "beads," for lack of a better term, are being found in significant amounts throughout the world, even in something as pristine as Arctic snow.[19]

---

17   https://www.forbes.com/sites/scottsnowden/2019/05/30/300-mile-swim-through-the-great-pacific-garbage-patch-will-collect-data-on-plastic-pollution/#29d43fd0489f

18   https://www.onegreenplanet.org/animalsandnature/marine-animals-are-dying-because-of-our-plastic-trash/

19   https://www.nationalgeographic.com/environment/2019/08/

Microplastics are appearing in soil and drinking water around the world. Studies have confirmed them to be in the air.[20] More than likely, that cup of coffee you are enjoying while reading this book contains some microplastics in the brew.[21] It's even showing up in human breast milk.[22] Your body reacts to ingested plastic in ways that are still being investigated. Some research shows it may lead to hormonal disruptions in both men and women.[23] If the possibility of a lowered testosterone level doesn't call men to action, I don't know what will.

Would it really be best to ban all plastic?

Plastic is not inherently evil. It is just another of humanity's inventions that can be beneficial if used properly or harmful if used carelessly or malevolently. I've already mentioned some of the positive aspects of plastic but, in the pursuit of fairness, I think more discussion is warranted.

The use of plastics has had a positive effect on some animal populations. Whale bone, elephant ivory, and tortoise shell have been replaced by plastic (although there is also a plant substitute for ivory in use). While whales, terrapins, and elephants are still threatened (some species are still critically endangered) plastics have provided manufacturers with a useful alternative material. These applications are not single-use.

microplastics-found-in-arctic-snow/

20   https://phys.org/news/2019-12-reveals-higher-microplastics-london-air.html?utm_source=nwletter&utm_medium=email&utm_campaign=daily-nwletter

21   https://www.epa.gov/sites/production/files/2018-03/documents/microplastics_expert_workshop_report_final_12-4-17.pdf

22   https://www.ncbi.nlm.nih.gov/pmc/articles/PMC4381877

23   https://www.ncbi.nlm.nih.gov/pmc/articles/PMC5832226/

Ever drop a glass bottle of shampoo in the shower? If you're under fifty you probably haven't. As far as you can remember, your toiletry products have always come in plastic containers, many of which are now recyclable. Plastic has provided an added level of safety. Seatbelts are made of nylon webbing and airbags are high-strength plastic. Both of these things save thousands of lives a year. Automotive safety glass, which is composed of plastic sandwiched between layers of glass, has been in use for decades, reducing serious injuries. Also, many medical devices would be impossible without plastic.

So, as we balance the need for and benefits of plastic against the harm, what solution can we determine? What is a concerned conservative's next move? You might say the answer is clear: let's ban all plastics. What else can we do? Mankind got along for centuries without it, so we'll be fine! But a ban would be an impractical solution.

The real answer is not as hard as you expect.

Everyone knows the best way to solve a problem is to prevent it from happening in the first place. There are a number of innovative companies and organizations that are looking to replace single-use plastics or limited-life products with non-toxic and easily recycled materials.

Hard Rock Stadium, home to the Miami Dolphins,[24] is eliminating plastic beverage cups from its concession stands. The old cups, which can be recycled (though not easily), are being replaced by a thin-gauge aluminum cup. Soft drink and beer companies have offered their product in aluminum cans

---

24   https://www.popularmechanics.com/science/a30297645/miami-hard-rock-stadium-plastic-free/

since shortly after World War II. Now they are also offering it in aluminum bottles.

Apple has been making its products with mostly aluminum frames for years. In 2018, all the aluminum came from recycled sources. To take it one step further, Apple recently took delivery of a shipment of recycled aluminum that was re-refined without carbon fuels.[25] Like many other technology product manufacturers, Apple contracts with recycling firms to take back and often pay the consumer for trading in their old products, such as phones and computers (more on this later).

Aluminum, which is one of the most easily recycled metals, is taking the place of plastics where conductivity is not an issue but light weight and strength are required.

Some other approaches are taken when it comes to plastic in manufacturing. For example, Dell Technologies (my employer during the time I wrote this book) has a plan to close the loop on the use of plastic materials. They reuse what they can in manufacturing and what they can't use they give to others who can. Regardless of the manufacturer of your computer, there are a lot of valuable materials built into it that are cheaper to recover and reuse than to obtain new.[26] This plan is to Dell's credit, for reusing plastic is not always the most economical approach in the short term; but half a pound of plastic sitting on your desk or in your data center is better for the environment and you than it is sitting in a landfill or floating across the Atlantic Ocean. Dell also partakes in an initiative to use plastic recovered from the

25   https://www.bizjournals.com/pittsburgh/news/2019/12/06/apple-buys-first-ever-carbon-free-aluminum-from.html

26   https://corporate.delltechnologies.com/en-us/social-impact/advancing-sustainability/sustainable-products-and-services/materials-use/recycled-materials.htm

ocean in some of their products. They hope to use tons of recovered material rather than new.[27]

Is recycling plastic even worth it?

The unfortunate thing about recycled materials, whether plastic, glass, metal, or paper, is that they merely become another commodity. This means they are subject to the same market forces as any other commodity. There may be times when it is cheaper not to recycle—and that's been the problem with plastic throughout its history. It may be cheaper to produce more virgin plastic than to gather, clean, transport, and reuse existing plastic. We are seeing this in China, where the appetite for the world's used plastic has nearly disappeared, leaving everyone else with piles of commodities that are more expensive to process for reuse than creating new plastic stocks would be.

One short-term-thinking columnist in the *Boston Herald* advocated abandoning plastic recycling efforts in favor of dumping used plastic into landfills. It's cheaper.[28] Unfortunately this solution will leave us with landfills brimming with a problem that won't go away in our lifetimes or for centuries to come.

So, who is ultimately responsible for this mess? Who *should* be responsible for it?

In my opinion, everyone. In his book *The Ecology of Commerce*, Paul Hawken points out that the real cost of a commodity isn't just the cost of materials, labor, and

---

27 https://www.recyclingtoday.com/article/refocus-2018-dell-ocean-bound-plastics-recycling/

28 http://bostonherald.ma.newsmemory.com/?publink=14e2459cd

overhead; it also includes the cost of the effects of misuse of the product and its ultimate disposal.[29]

I don't advocate taxing the producers of plastic or other difficult-to-recycle materials in order to fund that recycling process. Considering the bureaucratic framework that would be needed to assess, collect, and distribute this tax money, the real loser of the scenario would be the consumer. There would be inevitable waste, on top of the fact that there is no guarantee that the money would be directed toward its intended use.

The best approach is to reduce the overall amount of plastic entering the environment. As illustrated by the examples given earlier in this book, people just need to let companies and government know how they feel about finding substitutes for plastics and alternatives to single-use plastic products. The long term will result in less plastic in the environment. Maybe the cost of disposal of plastic items should be factored into their sale price. It would raise the price of many products—which would cause a shift to less harmful materials being used instead. Another option is to offer tax breaks to manufacturers who use recycled plastic in their products.

Reduction of plastic in the environment through the use of safer, less permanent materials may result in a shift on the same scale as the move *to* plastic in manufacturing fifty years ago.

---

29   Paul Hawken, The Ecology of Commerce: A Declaration of Sustainability, Harper Business (Collins Business Essentials), Kindle revised edition, 2013.

AN EAGLE OVER QUABBIN AND NEONICOTINOIDS

In the introduction I mentioned the wildlife that was familiar to me when I was growing up in a semi-rural part of Massachusetts. While there was a lot of wildlife, some species were missing. In particular, it was very rare to see a raptor. Of course, I didn't miss them; to me they were semi-exotic birds that were supposed to be found in faraway places, not the woods right outside my house.

I was too young to know about the seminal book *Silent Spring* by Rachel Carson when it was first published. According to her research, there was a serious drop in the population of raptors (an umbrella term for eagles, hawks, osprey, and others).[30] Among these birds that were fast disappearing was the bald eagle, the very symbol of the United States. It was perilously close to extinction. The disappearance of predatory birds could have led to some areas being overrun with crop-destroying rodents and other small mammals that are often

---

30   https://web.stanford.edu/group/stanfordbirds/text/essays/DDT_and_Birds.html

considered pests. Carson's work managed to get the use of DDT restricted, and this act was followed by a subsequent rebound in raptors' presence throughout North America.

Sixteen years after *Silent Spring* was published, I was on a picnic at the Quabbin Reservoir in western Massachusetts when I saw one of the first bald eagles to nest in Massachusetts in decades. Only then did I grasp the lesson that some of my high school science teachers were trying to drive home.

Why the trip down memory lane? Because, in my opinion, history is repeating itself. Only this time, the issue isn't the majestic raptors that hunt in the woods, fields, and lakes of the world. No, now I'm referring to what may appear to be a humbler natural aviator but one that may be an even more important part of the ecosystem: the bee.

When was the last time you saw a swarm of honeybees flitting over a flowering bush or patch of dandelions in a field? Even the wide-bodies of the apiary world, bumblebees, aren't as common as they once were. Over the past decade, several species of bees seem to have virtually disappeared from nature. As anyone who knows the basics of agriculture knows, bees provide a vital service. Without bees to pollinate, many of our most vital food crops will not grow. The result will be less food for humans.

It's not just the wild bees that are in trouble, either. Beekeepers are struggling to maintain their domestic hives, which are often let out to farmers to pollinate crops in fields and orchards. Crops which form a large part of human diets.

Bees are not the only pollinators

Natural pollination provided by bees and other pollinating creatures helps insure a bit of genetic diversity among crops. Such diversity helps plants survive against natural pests and unfavorable temperatures and weather conditions. Without it, you risk growing plants that are virtual clones.

So why are the bees disappearing? There's been a lot of research into this issue in the past decade. The accepted name for the discovered phenomenon is Colony Collapse Disorder, abbreviated CCD.[31] Much of the available evidence for CCD is pointing toward the use, or rather the overuse, of pesticides. One particular culprit is the pesticide class called neonicotinoids. Pesticides are such a worrisome issue that the EPA has issued additional guidelines as well as instructions for pesticide manufacturers to report the deaths of bees.[32]

My research references for this come directly from the EPA, which may conduct a lot of studies but, like many agencies of the federal government, can be maddeningly slow when it comes to following up with appropriate action. In contrast, the member nations of the European Union have voted to ban the use of neonicotinoids except under controlled situations, such as in greenhouses.

I'm sure many people are thinking that this powerful pesticide must only be available to licensed professionals. Unfortunately, that is not true. A search at your favorite online store or a stroll into a nearby big box store with a garden department will prove it readily available to anybody. Check any pesticide product label for the active ingredients, look up

---

31   https://www.epa.gov/pollinator-protection/colony-collapse-disorder
32   https://www.epa.gov/pollinator-protection/what-you-can-do-protect-honey-bees-and-other-pollinators

those ingredients, and you will probably see that some are classified as neonicotinoids.

Why is this class of pesticide so popular? For the simple reason that it is highly effective, as most insects are vulnerable to it. Agriculturalists will treat the seeds before sowing to render them toxic to the invertebrate pests. The soil is treated as well, and then the plants once sprouted. Since it is a systemic product, it is absorbed into the plants themselves; you can't wash it off of your fruits and vegetables.[33]

Unfortunately, the neurotoxins do not discriminate between helpful invertebrates and pests:

… Nanogram quantities of the neurotoxin are present in pollen and nectar and these pose sub-lethal risks to pollinators, such as bees. Nearby crop and wild plants can also be contaminated, and the insecticides can accumulate in soil. Neonics have been detected in streams, honey, garden flowers and wildflowers. It's not just bees, either. A Dutch study reported that birds raised fewer chicks when levels of imidacloprid were higher in surface waters. The more present, the poorer the fare of aquatic invertebrates. A review last year highlighted potential links to butterfly declines and harm to ants, earthworms, mayflies, and caddisflies.[34]

I could cite one study after another that points out the loss of insects and birds in North America and other parts of the world where neonicotinoids are in general use. These studies all seem to point toward this class of insecticides as the culprit. The sponsors and investigators of these studies vary widely, and their research is being made available online and in scientific journals—not only, as one might snidely

---

33   https://www.ncbi.nlm.nih.gov/pmc/articles/PMC4284396/

34   https://www.chemistryworld.com/news/what-you-need-to-know-about-neonicotinoids/3008816.article

joke, in the *Tree-Hugger Monthly*.[35] A quick web search can reveal even more information on this topic.

All this research seems to strengthen Rachel Carson's premise about silent killers like pesticides. The difference is that hers was regarding a since banned product, DDT. In my opinion, neonicotinoids are the DDT of the twenty-first century. In addition to the desirable invertebrates being eliminated by the misuse of pesticides, we seem to be losing other animals that depend on them for food.

Is a ban on neonicotinoids in order? Probably, or at least some serious restrictions. The retail sale of such products is of concern. People are notoriously lax when it comes to storing chemicals at home. Perhaps the reasoning is that, if it were dangerous, they wouldn't allow its sale to anyone who can walk into a retail store. (Unfortunately, we know that's not true.)

Eventually neonicotinoids should be removed from the market. While immediately would be best, I would not object to a phase-out over the course of several years. Such a plan would allow farmers and other agriculturalists a couple of seasons to test the effectiveness of less toxic alternatives.

There is legal and historic precedent for governmental regulatory agencies to ban dangerous products, and it may be time for the EPA to step in again.[36] Neonicotinoids and DDT have some things in common. When first introduced they were seen as nearly miraculous in their success. Controversy appeared after years of use as the effect on the environment became noticeable. The EPA's record of dragging its feet

---

35   A fictional publication to which an obstinate friend of mine attributes any environmentalism-related piece with which he disagrees.

36   https://www.epa.gov/ingredients-used-pesticide-products/ddt-brief-history-and-status

in both cases is, unfortunately, political and not based on research.

In the meantime, you can research the best ways to avoid products containing neonicotinoids. You can also check with your local parks departments to make sure that dangerous pesticides are not used in public parks and recreational fields. Get involved and let your local elected officials know your feelings.

ANOTHER BILL OF GOODS: GLYPHOSATE

For forty years the number one-selling broad-spectrum herbicide has been used all over the world, from Grandma's rose garden to tracts of agricultural land spanning hundreds of acres. Its chemical name is glyphosate. Right now, you're probably saying, "Huh, never heard of it." Okay, no one can blame you for that, but you must have heard the trade name: Roundup.

Monsanto came up with a plan to make the use of Roundup even more effective for farmers who developed food crops that were resistant to glyphosate. As a capitalist and conservative, I would normally applaud such creative thinking. It's extremely beneficial that our crops are resistant to the chemicals designed to kill interlopers in the fields where they grow. This reduces the labor required to apply the chemicals, as there's no need to be selective in the process.

According to the label on the bottle, glyphosate is, more or less, benign. We are told that the chemical breaks down in the soil and is harmless to humans. These claims are under review with the EPA, however, as there is some evidence that glyphosate is a possible carcinogen in mammals.[37]

It's worth noting that over the years the problem develops—as happens with neonicotinoids—that glyphosate becomes less effective due to its targets developing a resistance to it. Just as bacteria develop a resistance to antibiotics and insects develop a resistance to pesticides, unwanted plants (i.e. weeds) develop a resistance to glyphosate.

One way to deal with any issue where resistance is being built up is to become more selective in the use of the substance in question. As doctors are now encouraged to do with antibiotics, agriculturalists should with their chemicals: Identify the specific threat or threats and prescribe specific, directed treatments. Just as the medical world is dealing with the aftermath of generations of bacteria that became resistant, farmers have to deal with the problem of resistant weeds overrunning their fields as well as the difficulty of pollinating their crops (the natural pollinators are no longer around because of the broad spectrum of insecticides and herbicides used over time).

An argument against the restriction or outright ban of certain agricultural chemicals can be made in that they allow more crops per acre, with less loss to pests and without unwanted plants competing for nutrients and water. I don't think the current processes that are referred to as sustainable will scale up to the same level of modern agricultural practices. The solution lies somewhere in between and will only be found when science and economics balance out.

---

37   https://search.epa.gov/epasearch/?querytext=&areaname=&areacontacts=&areasearchurl=&typeofsearch=epa&result_template=2col.ftl#/

Cap-and-trade deals with chemicals

One solution to the use, or more accurately overuse, of agricultural chemicals may be to adopt a cap-and-trade option similar to those that have been used to address other environmental issues. As discussed a little later in this book, this would involve an agreement between the companies making neonicotinoids and glyphosate, the users of the products, the appropriate regulatory agencies, and consumers. They might set a certain usage limit for a target year and then offer incentives and alternative methods of pest and weed control—perhaps non-chemical alternatives. It would also be reasonable to offer something akin to renewable energy credits to organic farmers and others using methods of weed and pest control that are generally regarded as safe.

CARBON OFFSETS AND RENEWABLE ENERGY CREDITS

A serious issue that was first talked about in earnest in the 1980s was acid rain. Because of high-sulfur fuels being burned by industry and electrical utilities, large amounts of pollutants (including sulfur) were released into the atmosphere. This resulted in various parts of the country—of the globe, for that matter—experiencing precipitation with measurably lower pH level than it should have had, due to the sulfur gasses and vapor in their clouds. When the vapor condensed into rain a weak, but noticeable, sulfuric acid fell with the rain. Many forested areas were damaged, lakes and rivers became poisonous to fish and amphibians, and crops suffered.

People at the EPA realized that they could not just ban the use of high-sulfur fuels outright—there was no economical way to clean the emissions. So, as a compromise, a cap-and-trade system was developed to reduce the acid in the rain.

How does cap and trade work in relation to this issue? Well, the governing authority sets the limits (the "cap"), allocates to each current polluter, and gradually lowers the limits. And then of course there is the "trade" part: Companies that pay for the tech to reduce their emissions are allowed to trade or sell to other companies some of their allocation of pollution. It is a truly capitalistic way to solve a problem. (Cap and trade may also be the solution to problems with carbon dioxide and methane emissions.)

Carbon offsets require specific provable actions to certify that they exist. This could be a company switching from diesel trucks to hybrids, thereby reducing their use of carbon-based diesel fuel. Or the same company could switch to diesel from renewable sources like waste vegetable oil or algae (which is still experimental). In any case, such actions allow the company to claim carbon offsets which can then be sold, traded, or used to offset the carbon consumed in another of its projects, such as building a new campus or expanding its current facilities.

Carbon offsets are also bought by companies to become greener in their own daily operation when it is not technically feasible to do so at the moment. For example, a railroad or a long-haul trucking company may not be able to find a suitable substitute for its diesel fuel; but by purchasing carbon offsets, they can claim to be a greener company.[38]

Closely related to carbon offsets are renewable energy credits, or RECs. One REC is generated for every megawatt of electricity generated from a renewable source. Some of the obvious renewable energy sources are solar, hydro reflection, and wind power. Once the system is installed, the generated electricity neither consumes nor produces carbon. The more energy produced, the more RECs an organization has to

---

38   https://www.epa.gov/sites/production/files/2018-03/documents/gpp_guide_recs_offsets.pdf

sell. This can be used to finance more projects or to pay the investors who paid to build the generation facilities. There can be money in being green.

How do I get in on this?

Now you're wondering if an individual can buy carbon offsets or RECs. The answer is yes—but it's not always easy.

Some offsets are better than others. For instance, if you pay money to an organization that pays landowners not to cut down a forest, that is very different from buying offsets from an organization that uses the money to reforest a denuded area. The former is being passive in maintaining the world's carbon-sequestering capability. The latter is working to actually remove carbon from the atmosphere. If you are looking for a way to reduce your net carbon footprint (sorry, I was really going to try and not use that term) then buying carbon offsets may be the way to go.

I'm not qualified to offer financial advice, but if this is something that you may wish to investigate further. Talk to your accounting or tax professional. Under certain circumstances the carbon offsets you purchase may be tax deductible. When I was researching this, I saw that if you purchase offsets offered by 501(c)(3) corporations, then you can deduct the cost. With carbon offsets it becomes possible to take that flight to Europe and not cause a net increase in the level of carbon dioxide in the atmosphere.

It is also possible to purchase RECs. Most individuals who buy RECs do so through their local electricity provider. This is a result of a much criticized (at the time) 1992 law that deregulated the energy market. This act, similar to the deregulation of the telephone industry some years earlier, allowed for the separation of electricity-related services for the individual consumer. The same company that generates your electricity may not be the company that moves it over long distances and then handles its local or retail distribution.

This is an oversimplification, but in many cases, your friendly local utility company may be buying electricity from multiple sources which may be located hundreds or thousands of miles from your meter.

As part of the process and probably a positive, albeit unintended, result of it, you can choose your generating company; you need not use the same company that maintains the lines going into your home.

It was assumed that many people would begin choosing the cheapest power available. It's electricity, a commodity. One watt is the same as the other, right? What has actually happened is that a significant amount of people needing electricity are concerned about the environment. The paradox of choosing electric heat for your home and driving an electric car but knowing that the electricity provided by your local utility company has been produced from a coal or natural gas generator is a problem for some people.

Due to the right to choose who generates their power, customers can indicate that they want to buy power from a non-carbon-using renewable source. The usual choices are hydro power, solar, or wind, or perhaps a combination of all three. The result is that you are not only using renewable power, but you are helping to support the producers of such power.

Since there is one nationwide grid for power, the electricity you are receiving is from a mix of sources. The RECs are an entry in a ledger. But the result is what you want: Through your personal utility spending, renewable energy is being supported and unsustainable power generation is not.

Again, I am not giving tax or financial advice. Any special tax treatment questions you may have regarding REC purchases should be handed by your professional advisor.

There are some utility customers who won't be able to participate in the purchase of RECs. The deregulation of the electricity market exempted municipal or otherwise publicly owned utilities from the requirement that its members or customers be able choose their sources of electricity.

When electricity deregulation went into effect the predictions were mass bankruptcies, rolling blackouts, and poorer service in general. None of these materialized. As a matter of fact, there are more choices than ever for most electric utility customers—at least, up until that last mile of delivery to your home.

THE QUEST FOR ENERGY

One thing that will never change about our world is our thirst for energy. Mankind has relied on some form of external energy or another since we discovered how to make fire and used it for beneficial purposes such as warming ourselves, keeping predators at bay, and, eventually, cooking.

As the millennia progressed, our needs grew. We cut millions of square miles of forest for wood, tamed streams for hydropower to directly power machines that milled grain and powered industrial machines, used the wind to power machines that pumped water to reclaim land, dug holes in the ground for rocks that burned, and drilled holes for crude oil and gas.

Fortunes were made and lost looking for and retrieving fossil fuels. Wars were, and still are, fought and lives lost over fossil fuels. These fights weren't just between nations but also between mine owners and miners. The West Virginia coal wars are just one example of this.[39]

---

39   http://www.wvculture.org/history/archives/minewars.html

Electricity is clean, but its generation may not be.

In the twentieth century we figured out how to use atoms and the sun to further power our lives. The new technology has done little to stop global conflicts over energy.

Some of our new technologies show the potential of adding to available power, but they are only now making inroads. And one class of technology that showed so much promise a half century ago now makes people nervous at the mere sound of its name. And then there is another class of technology that inspires science fiction writers and contemporary physicists alike: nuclear fusion.

Recently, a town in Massachusetts decided to make electricity the de facto household form of energy. Brookline has mandates in its building code which ban gas or oil connections in new construction. They eliminated the consumers' choice for energy. Electricity is the only form of heat allowed (though fireplaces are permitted).[40] Geothermal power is not banned, but that is not an option in many areas.

This chapter is a discussion of the various forms of energy that humans have used and are using today. It will also touch briefly on a futuristic form of energy that is the dream of many physicists. No form of energy used by human beings is perfectly safe, perfectly clean, or perfectly reliable. There is good and bad to each of the many forms of energy that civilization has developed and relied upon over the centuries. The decision must be made: Which are going to power our future and which will remain in our past?

---

40   https://www.bostonglobe.com/metro/2019/11/20/first-for-massachusetts-brookline-votes-ban-oil-and-gas-pipes-new-buildings/24RdqjUOldI5qrqF6zfiHP/story.html

Wood

No one knows for sure when human beings or their immediate precursors discovered a way to create and control wood fires for their benefits. An incredible technical achievement, fire kept our ancestors warm and frightened off predators that may have been waiting in the shadows to pounce on their weak and relatively defenseless prey. The use of a wood fire enabled food to be cooked, which scientists now tell us makes food easier to digest, giving early man more energy per meal as the body expended less on digestion.

Wood suited man's energy needs for millennia. The supply in many areas seemed endless, it was locally produced, and it was simple to use. It didn't require engineers to come up with ways to gather it. While the world's population of human beings was relatively small, wood could be considered renewable. A pioneer family in North America with a few hundred acres of woods on their property would probably go for generations with the supply their trees afforded—provided they were trying to meet only their own energy needs and not supply everyone in town with wood.

Wood provided a stable and easily transportable fuel. Although coal started to become more readily available in the early nineteenth century, wood was still in use for many applications. For example, when Robert Fulton built the North River Steamboat, later dubbed the Clermont, it was powered by pinewood.[41]

Wood was still the primary source for heating when the first railroads started crossing the landscape. In fact, the last

---

41   Mary Bellis, "The Steamboat Clermont," ThoughtCo, Nov. 20, 2019. thoughtco.com/steamboat-clermont-1991465.

wood-burning railroad locomotive was built as late as 1928.[42] Wood was slowly replaced with coal as the nineteenth century advanced. Coal was becoming cheaper as more mines opened up and technology for digging deeper into the earth and getting better quality coal made it less expensive to produce than wood.

Although wood is still used for some residential heating purposes, including modified versions (in the form of pellets), wood has largely been replaced as a day-to-day fuel in most of the developed world.

Advocates of wood and other biomass as a fuel often claim it is a renewable resource. I would take exception to that, as do some experts. Since it takes decades to replace trees burned as fuel and it is not instantly renewable as is solar, wind, or hydro power, it cannot really be labeled renewable in a short-term sense.

There is also the carbon neutrality question, although any carbon released by burning wood has been sequestered in the past few decades and it will take decades of tree growth to recapture an equivalent amount of carbon.

I don't see wood being a viable alternative to other forms of fuel anymore, as mentioned, because a tree takes so long to grow and many environmental groups and energy experts don't consider wood to be a renewable resource. The same professional opinion seems to apply regarding the sister of wood-burning energy sources, biomass.

Wood does enjoy occasional resurgence in popularity as a fuel, but this usually occurs when there are spikes in heating oil or natural gas prices. Only two percent of American households use wood as a primary heat source.[43] A much

---

42   https://www.trainorders.com/discussion/read.php?10,3341843
43   http://www.forgreenheat.org/background/america.html

larger percentage of homes may have fireplaces, wood stoves, or pellet systems as a secondary heat source.

Did coal and oil save forests?

A few years ago, when looking at old pictures of rural towns (usually pre-1930 or so) I noticed something: There aren't a lot of trees in them. Specifically, I was looking at photos of tourist sites and early ski areas in New Hampshire. In these photos I saw buildings that still stand today. I saw neatly landscaped hotel grounds, ski resorts, town parks, and lakes. Any trees that were visible in the photos tended to be relatively young ones, maybe less than twenty or thirty years old. I began to speculate, but haven't proven, that twenty to thirty years prior to the pictures being taken there were very few trees around because they were all being used for fuel. What are now nearby forests and small copses were often fields. New Hampshire's mountains had already had many of their larger trees cut down for use as timber to be used in construction and for fuel.

Strangely, the world's conversion to coal as a primary source for heat at home and in transportation and industry may have helped to save forests and other wooded areas. It became cheaper to mine and transport coal than it did to cut and haul wood out of a forest. The mining of coal scaled up much more easily than the cutting of lumber. Railroads made it economical to move coal from remote areas. While wood remains the primary building material in the United States, its popularity as a fuel has waned to single digits in terms of percentage of homes heated.

Coal had been known to mankind for centuries, but coal mining in North America really took off in the middle of the nineteenth century as rich veins of high-quality coal were discovered in Pennsylvania and what was then part of Virginia. In addition to providing efficient heat and relatively easy transportation, it didn't attract chipmunks when piled outdoors. Also, a ton of coal provides a lot more heat than a ton of wood. Another factor in the adoption of coal for industry is that factories no longer had to be located along rivers and streams to power machinery. Locally produced steam heat provided mechanical power and later electrical power for factories and shops.

The Department of Energy has a concise study guide of the history of coal. Admittedly, it's aimed toward younger readers, but it is nonetheless informative.[44]

With all the positives aspects of coal—high energy density, deposits that will last centuries, versatility—coal would be the perfect fuel if it weren't for a few issues.

Burning coal releases carbon dioxide and numerous dangerous elements, sulfur and mercury among them. It leaves behind toxic ash that creates additional environmental hazards. And as much as coal-burning entities try to prevent it, the contaminants from power plants leach chemicals into nearby bodies of water and the water table.

A serious issue that is seldom brought up when coal is discussed by its advocates is that coal mining is one of the most dangerous professions in the world. Coal miners die every year from causes ranging from direct mining accidents to cardio-pulmonary issues and cancers that can take years to develop.

Dirty and dangerous—two hardly appealing characteristics upon which to base an economy. Yet very few U.S. states are

---

44   https://www.energy.gov/sites/prod/files/Elem_Coal_Studyguide.pdf

without coal-burning power plants. And those of us who reside in states with no coal-fired plants shouldn't feel smug; it's all one big grid, so chances are you are using coal-derived power anyway.

Many conservatives, dare I say all, eschew any large, established industry receiving government subsidies for anything that is already highly profitable. Yet, the federal government still provides millions, if not billions, of dollars in subsidies to the coal industry.[45] This is mostly for electricity generation purposes. Very little is actually spent on developing technology to work with the myth of clean coal. The subsidies also consist of legitimate tax write-offs for depleting reserves. This is a credit offered to any mining or drilling operation or other commodity producer.

Oil

As is the case with coal, people around the world knew about petroleum for centuries but considered its uses very limited—that is, until the Industrial Revolution and the development of economical extraction and refining methods.

Much of the history between the last decades of the nineteen century and the beginning of the twenty-first century is directly tied to oil: its exploration, transportation, control of the nations where it was found, and later the independence of those nations. Historians will argue that the refusal of the United States to sell oil to Japan was one of the rationalizations for the attack on Pearl Harbor and the attempt to drive the U.S. out of the Pacific theater.

---

45   https://www.eia.gov/analysis/requests/subsidy/

One of the largest corporations ever (in terms adjusted for inflation) was Standard Oil. It was a virtual monopoly for the exploration, drilling, transportation, refinement, and retail sales for what was becoming, excuse the cliché, the lifeblood of the American economy and the rest of the industrialized world. One of the reasons President Theodore Roosevelt earned a place in our national memory is for recognizing the danger of any one corporation controlling an essential material such as oil.[46]

Since the focus of this book is conservation of the planet, I won't get involved in the morality and motives of all the domestic and international intrigue that has revolved around securing the rights, legitimately and otherwise, to recover and move oil. If you are interested in the history of the subject I recommend Daniel Yergin's *The Prize*, a history book that reads like a novel as it follows the worldwide thirst for oil.[47]

Petroleum-based fuels are also among the dirtiest; only coal is dirtier. Oil requires extraction from below ground, transportation to refineries, and refining before it can be of use. All of these processes require even more energy.

Oil is recovered from oil fields located from the Arctic to the tip of South America and in just about every climate in between. In addition to a liquid being pumped from the ground, oil is also recovered from tar sands and shale deposits. In the latest move to make the most out of oil deposits, a practice of fracturing bedrock and injecting wastewater in one form or another into the ground and pumping out a mixture of the water and crude oil is being used all around North America. This practice is making the United States

---

46   Roosevelt also went after the steel industry.

47   Daniel Yergin, The Prize, Simon & Schuster, 1991.

a net exporter of oil and virtually energy independent. It is referred to in the vernacular as fracking.

Unfortunately, fracking comes with a cost. As earlier written, the business of oil recovery and transportation is dirty. Shale deposits and tar sands relinquish oil, but they leave a mess behind. Fracking is suspected of causing drinking water pollution and has been suspected in a number of earthquakes, especially in areas where earthquakes used to be a rarity. Research is still ongoing.

The most efficient way to transport oil over land is through pipelines. Because oil is found in more and more remote locations, the pipelines are sometimes routed through environmentally sensitive locations or areas of cultural importance.

As an aside: I'd feel rather hypocritical to protest the placement of pipelines or potentially dangerous recovery methods of oil. I drive a car that uses gasoline and live in a home heated, as many are in the northeastern U.S., by oil—essentially diesel oil. Instead, maybe my best course of action would be to encourage through investments and commercial incentives to push for cleaner forms of energy to replace what we use.

The biggest provider of energy is probably the most subsidized. In addition to the usual federal and state tax breaks and allowances for depreciation and depletion,[48] there is the hidden subsidy that comes through the Department of Defense. The subsidy isn't paid directly but rather it's in the billions in defense dollars from the cost of the navy guarding the shipping lanes, military aid sent to allies to keep them as allies, and satellites covering the skies.

---

48   https://www.eesi.org/papers/view/fact-sheet-fossil-fuel-subsidies-a-closer-look-at-tax-breaks-and-societal-costs

Oil is more than a source of energy. Oil provides the raw materials for plastics and chemicals and is used for mechanical lubrication. Helium was once seen as useless byproduct of oil production, but its industrial value was soon recognized in the early twentieth century. For these reasons, we will probably not see an end to oil production in our lifetimes.

Natural gas

Natural gas is another fossil fuel. Composed mainly of methane with traces of other gases, it is considered a cleaner alternative, for some purposes, to other fossil fuels. In the early days of oil exploration until the early part of the twentieth century, natural gas was released into the atmosphere, as there was no way to efficiently collect it and transport it to where it could be used.

Technical improvements have made feasible the recovery and transportation of gas that used to be discarded, though some is still wasted. Even today natural gas is sometimes allowed to burn off at oil refineries when it is considered either not in great enough quantity or of too low a quality to be commercially viable.

In North America natural gas has been replacing oil and coal in power plants. Fleets of commercial vehicles have converted to natural gas from diesel. In my area, the trash and recycling collection trucks are now powered by natural gas. They are better for residential areas, as they are quieter and emit less noxious fumes than their diesel counterparts. Some automobile and light truck manufacturers offer natural gas versions of their gasoline-powered models. At this time, they do not represent a large portion of the nation's fleet, however.

Cars powered by natural gas are usually part of a commercial fleet.

The conversion to natural gas from oil and coal is because of new extraction technologies. Estimates of the usable reserves of natural gas have risen in the past ten years.

Like oil, natural gas also some commercial and industrial uses in the chemical industry. Pennzoil, for example, has developed a synthetic motor oil that is made from natural gas. So, like petroleum, it will still be a valuable commodity even if better and cheaper alternative forms of energy are found.

Cleaner ways to get electricity

Biomass and fossil fuels are dirty, but is clean electricity possible?

Waterpower

When discussing the reversal of environmental damage, this book touched earlier on the usefulness of the Blackstone River as a source of power in central Massachusetts and Rhode Island. Waterpower was important to the industrialization of the United States, particularly in the Northeast.

At the time of Samuel Slater, factories had to be built near rivers since the power they provided was purely the kinetic energy of water converted to mechanical power. There was no conversion to electricity that would eventually be called hydroelectric power. Towns and villages in the region even had names derived from description of the water flowing through them: Attleborough Falls, Central Falls, and Fall

River are just a few. In some areas the water was channeled into man-made ponds or lakes, often referred to as reservoirs, so they could control the flow of water year-round and not be at the mercy of seasonal fluctuations which could result in too high or too low a flow of water, which in turn would affect production in the factories.

Compared to modern hydropower projects, ponds, dams, and channels were modest; but they effectively demonstrated that waterpower could be used for more than just grinding grain at the mill.

The twentieth and twenty-first century hydro projects have been massive. Dams in the western United States that represented engineering milestones were the forerunners to massive regional projects controlled by the Tennessee Valley Authority and the dozens of projects controlled by Hydro Quebec, producing electrical power for large parts of Canada and the United States. But the largest hydroelectric power installation in the world is the Three Gorges Dam on the Yangtze River in China. Large-scale hydroelectric power projects can make clean electrical power available to customers hundreds or thousands of miles away. A consumer of hydropower doesn't have to be abutting a body of water.

According to industry sources, hydropower is seven percent of the total electrical power generated in the United States. It represents fifty-two percent of the renewable energy used.[49] There are plans to build more hydro plants in the U.S. and to bring more hydropower into the New England region. Massachusetts looks to be a big customer for the Canadian-produced power.

---

49   https://www.hydro.org/waterpower/why-hydro/available/

All of this sounds pretty good, terawatts of power produced without the introduction of greenhouse gases into the atmosphere. It's not without controversy, however. Mega hydro projects have displaced people, swallowed towns, obliterated archeological sites, and wreaked havoc with the ecosystems both upstream and downstream. In the case of the Three Gorges Dam, the weight of the water may have actually introduced a very slight change in the Earth's rotation.[50]

The dams themselves aren't the only controversy surrounding hydro projects. For years, residents of New Hampshire and Maine have complained about and protested proposed routes for power lines from the province of Quebec to the Commonwealth of Massachusetts.[51]

Solar power

The concept around solar power is fairly simple; the complexity revolves around installing it and dealing with the weather. The sun can be used to heat water into steam to run generators or be converted directly into electricity using photovoltaic cells. Photovoltaic activity has been known for nearly 200 years. It became a little more practical in the late 1950s when Bell Labs developed solar powered cells for use on satellites.[52] The most dramatic depiction of solar cells in use is on the International Space Station, one of the most complex feats of human engineering. The eight "wings" of the ISS have a combined total of nearly 35,000 square feet of solar panels providing between 84 and 120 kilowatts of

---

50   https://interestingengineering.com/13-facts-about-the-controversial-massive-chinese-dam-that-slowed-the-earths-rotation
51   https://www.outdoors.org/conservation/hot-issues/northern-pass
52   FIND REFERENCE

electricity, depending on the angle of the panels in relation to the sun. This could power about forty homes. The ISS does have the advantage of being well above the atmosphere. If any sort of clouds were obscuring their access to the sun, we would have a whole different set of issues to discuss.

Photovoltaic cells are appearing on rooftops all over the world, proving the practicality of the technology. It is getting cheaper and more efficient and makes use of otherwise unused space, i.e., millions of square feet of commercial and residential rooftops.

But the big question you ask as an individual is, how long will it be before you break even or start to make money off of your investment? How long will it be until you actually come out ahead? Well, let me first ask you this—how long do you think you'll be in your current residence? The value of solar panels, as far as the resale of your house, like anything else, may not increase proportionately with the money you've spent.

Solar panels are also being set up in large unused expanses of land. As you drive along an interstate highway you may see former farm pastures filled with acres of panels. Some cities and towns are also using capped landfills or former brownfield sites to add more energy to the grid.

Another approach to using solar energy is using the sun to directly heat a fluid. The most basic example of this approach is a solar water heater. During the energy crisis of the 1970s, many local utilities launched pilot programs for conservation and reduction of energy uses. One was the installation of solar water heaters on customers' rooftops. In my neighborhood, one of these is still in use in a small ranch-style home. This type of solar collector was used to provide hot water to a house or apartment. Water that would otherwise have been heated with oil, gas, or electricity.

Advanced solar boilers don't necessarily have to use water as a heat-conducting medium. One experimental solar boiler used sodium as its medium. The design featured a ring of mirrors that would focus sunlight onto a tower through which flowed liquefied sodium. While the design worked, the results weren't quite up to expectations. It did, however, demonstrate the potential for media besides water to be of use in solar boilers and for sodium as a coolant.[53]

A side comment on residential solar power

There are organizations that will install solar panels on your rooftop for a fraction of the retail cost. For this, the organization receives the benefit of the tax credits and depreciation of the capital investments. The owner of the building gets the credit from the local utility company for the power generated. My problem with this arrangement is that the organization is pretty much leasing your rooftop. You don't own the equipment. Before engaging in such an arrangement be certain to read and understand who is responsible for any problems caused by the equipment, what happens to ownership in the event the contract should be terminated—all the usual stuff that one would go through when spending a lot of money on something that is expected to last decades. Talk to a financial advisor.

---

53   https://www.popularmechanics.com/technology/a30472835/crescent-dunes-solar-plant/

Wind

Renewable energy discussion would not be nearly complete without a discussion of wind power. For centuries wind provided a renewable, completely carbon-free energy source for transportation and other purposes, such as drawing water from wells and reclaiming thousands of acres of land in low-lying nations like the Netherlands. In the United States today, wind power provides two percent of total electricity generated.

Modern wind turbines have become a symbol for clean and renewable energy. Everyone has seen television commercials where energy companies try to prove their commitment to the environment by showing hundreds of wind turbines lining miles of hillside or shallow ocean waters, quietly spinning and sending megawatts of power into the grid for the nation to use.

If you detected a slightly skeptical edge to the previous paragraph, you're not wrong. In some regions wind turbines have met with strong opposition. People in rural areas or with oceanview properties have objected to their installation because while they may be picturesque in their own way, many feel they are an eyesore. There is also debate as to the effects of the turbines' noise. Yes, some are noisy, causing unpleasantness and even danger to people and wildlife, especially birds. The rise and fall of the Cape Wind Project, a huge emplacement of turbines along the coast of Nantucket Island off of Massachusetts, has become the stuff of local legend. People blame the elite, both liberals and conservatives, who complained about the view from their multi-million-dollar beach homes being ruined. Fishermen and other maritime interests were worried about the effects on their livelihoods. The fate of Cape Wind could be the subject of an entire book, but for an energy-hungry New England, it was seen as the ultimate NIMBY issue.

Noise and wildlife issues aside, wind power is good source of power. Detractors will always point out that there may be calm days, and that's true, but there are places where the wind is pretty steady all the time, and downtime may be factored into the calculations of capacity. Two issues indirectly related to wind turbines that will be difficult to resolve are the amount of land they take up and the difficult-to-recycle turbine blades that have to be periodically replaced.

Nuclear fission

Just like every other form of energy, nuclear energy is mired in controversy. Nuclear power went from science fiction to reality in the 1940s, a product of decades of research and development. Its patrons were sidetracked by World War II and turned to a new specialty: developing nuclear weapons. The world was in awe of single device that could level the greater part of a city. Then came the positive aspects of nuclear power: It sent a submarine under the Arctic ice and then around the world without surfacing. There was talk of atomic energy sending rockets on interplanetary missions, airplanes that could stay aloft for weeks without refueling, home electricity too cheap to meter. The potential for nuclear power seemed limitless.

In the shadows, there was anxiety over its origins. Headline events like the Chernobyl, Pennsylvania's Three Mile Island, and most recently, the power plants at Fukushima have contributed to the anxiety of nuclear power.

Organized opposition to nuclear energy began in earnest in the early 1970s with the group Greenpeace which made headlines by trying to stop American nuclear weapons testing by sailing right into the testing area in defiance of the Coast Guard. Greenpeace then expanded their mission into fighting whaling, on which topic I agree with them, as well as nuclear power plants. There are some who think the broadened focus of their mission has hurt them.

Not everyone within Greenpeace necessarily agreed on the opposition to nuclear energy. One person changing their mind on an issue is not usually considered a big deal, of course. Times and circumstances change, and both those things can effect someone's position on an issue to change; but when the founder of one of the most vocally anti-nuclear power organizations states publicly that he is re-examining his position on nuclear power, people take notice. Such is the case with Greenpeace cofounder Patrick Moore.[54] I don't know Mr. Moore, but from what I've read he has come to feel that we need to take another look at nuclear generation, and he is not alone.

Not every nuclear power plant is a mega-complex with multiple cooling towers, or rather it doesn't have to be. There have been numerous proposals and innovations in the nuclear power industry for rethinking or redesigning nuclear power plants. Proposed ideas include differences in sizes, fuel manufacturing, and even fuel type itself. Some variations proposed for fission:

- Small-scale reactors
- Pebble reactors
- Thorium reactors that do not use uranium (thorium is radioactive but cannot be weaponized)

---

54   https://www.politico.com/story/2008/03/why-a-greenpeace-co-founder-went-nuclear-008835

- Passive cooling systems that would not require power to cool but the cooling would be a default in the design
- Conversion of nuclear waste into batteries is in the works for small-scale electrical power

I believe the future of nuclear power need not involve multi-billion-dollar investment in a single plant. With creative engineering, safe, small plants may power individual neighborhoods and small towns.

Nuclear fusion

Fusion is a form of energy that still seems firmly lodged in the realm of science fiction. Movies and television programs show fusion-powered spacecraft transiting the solar system, even the galaxy, at near the speed of light. There are those who dream of producing electricity here on Earth the way it's produced by the sun—through the fusion of hydrogen atoms into helium atoms. The intent is to make use of the heat that is released in the fusion process.

We have managed to generate fusion reactions on this planet by way of the hydrogen bomb, which has been with us since the 1950s. While the energy released is massive, so is its destructive power. We can create a fusion reaction that can destroy a city, but we can't control and harness it to power that city.

In spite of decades of research, no one has been able to create a sustained and controlled fusion reaction that produces more energy than it takes to start the reaction. Another problem with fusion reactions, if sustainability could be achieved, would be containing the heat generated. There is no material on Earth that could contain the heat of a fusion reactor. The reigning theory is to contain the reaction in a magnetic field of some sort.

In spite of these obstacles there may still be a future for nuclear fusion on Earth. The U.S. Navy filed a patent on what may be a miniature fusion reactor.[55] Its practicality has yet to be proven, but I believe science will overcome its obstacles. It will just take time.[56]

The future of electrical power

Electricity will continue to be a vital source of power for centuries to come, but how we generate it must change. I know most conservatives, myself included, loathe the idea of excessive taxpayer subsidies for private for-profit businesses, but the playing field should at least be leveled. I know many of my fellow conservatives will say that if a non-fossil fuel form of energy is such a great idea, then subsidies shouldn't be needed. That's the same argument I use when there's talk of a taxpayer-funded venue for a professional sports team. Perhaps if the use of public lands and the protection of tankers by the U.S. military were charged back to energy companies at a fair rate, the real costs of oil, gas, and coal would be realized.

Leases and mineral rights contracts between energy companies and their state and local governments should be examined. Does the tax law give the most breaks to the dirtiest sources of energy? Are special interest groups preventing the wind and solar industry from having the same access to

55   https://atomicinsights.com/did-us-navy-patent-a-functional-fusion-device/
56   https://cleantechnica.com/2019/10/14/did-the-us-navy-solve-clean-energy-with-a-compact-fusion-reactor/

federally owned land as hydro-generating companies?

The other problem with the use of fossil fuels versus cleaner forms of energy is dealing with the waste generated, be it ash, smoke, or carbon dioxide. We all have to live with the effects to the environment in general and to our individual health in particular.

I want to make a final push for nuclear power. Do some research into this groundbreaking energy source. You will find some fascinating information about new designs, different fuels, and cooling systems which can make the use of nuclear power even safer.

Calculation of the cost of energy has to take into account the amount of carbon released into the atmosphere. The goal is carbon neutrality, i.e. using an energy source that generates no additional carbon.

To close this topic: I don't intend my criticisms of alternative energy sources to be arguments against them. A megawatt of wind-generated energy is a lot healthier for all of us than a megawatt from a coal plant. Even though I am a fan of nuclear power from modern reactors and someday maybe fusion; a friend mentioned a quote that hits home now, more than ever;

"I'd put my money on the sun and solar energy. What a source of power! I hope we don't have to wait until oil and coal run out before we tackle that." *–Thomas Edison, 1931*

Who am I to doubt the man who brought practical electrical power to the world?

⁂

Physical footprints on the land

It's impossible to have a discussion, debate, or rant about energy usage these days in which the abstract concept of carbon footprint doesn't come up. The ongoing dialogue about energy, however, often leaves out any mention of the actual footprints of energy production.

A company called Strata Energy did some research on the concept of how much land is required per megawatt of energy generated and published a paper titled, "The Footprint of Energy: Land Use of U.S. Electricity Production," with their findings.[57] Among the surprising information the paper contains is this tidbit: Of the major sources of fuel for electric power generation, fossil fuels take up the least amount of real estate per megawatt of electricity generated, yet generate most of the pollutants. The cleanest forms of energy take up the most real estate, yet generate far fewer byproducts.

When considering the real estate factor in solar, wind, and hydro energy production, the installation of such systems has some negative environmental effects. Hundreds of acres of land to house solar panels will disrupt the local biome. Meanwhile hydro projects change geography, flood dry areas, and reduce water to places downstream, where toxins can build in the silt that forms behind dams.

◂ı|||ı▸

Transportation: How do alternative fuels stack up for motor vehicles?

---

57   This paper as well as other energy-related publications are available on their website www.strata.org.

The following is this book's most obvious statement yet: Americans are in love with their cars.

We have been for decades and will be for decades to come. From the Beach Boys' "Fun, Fun, Fun" to Meatloaf's "Paradise by the Dashboard Light," generations have come to identify the personal automobile as a symbol of freedom, not just in the sense of easy transportation but also from the restrictions of parental supervision and the promise of pending adulthood. No amount of planning, cajoling, or regulation will destroy that piece of the American spirit. But it doesn't mean that certain aspects of it can't change.

The personal automobile is ever evolving. I own a turbo-charged SUV that gets better mileage than a 1972 Volkswagen Super Beetle. It's also quieter, more comfortable, air conditioned, and has satellite radio— something VW engineers could only dream of for their vehicles in the 1970s.

Building on the prior discussion of the pros and cons of different energy sources, this chapter will examine alternative ways to power our personal vehicles. It's been gasoline for more than a century, but changes are coming. The question is, which fuel will dominate the automobile industry for the remainder of the twenty-first century?

Biodiesel

There is a cottage industry out there of people who are making their own diesel analog from waste vegetable oil obtained from restaurant kitchens. This product can be used in existing diesel engines as well as home heating systems with little or no modification of the existing equipment. I did some research into this and found it is a time-consuming process as well as messy and a little dangerous. It's best to set up your biodiesel kit in a well-ventilated outbuilding on your property. If you aren't familiar with the chemistry behind the process, then further education in chemistry and industrial safety may be in order.

Some of the chemicals you need for catalyst are the same as those needed to produce illegal methamphetamine. If you purchase significant amounts of these chemicals make sure you keep your documentation handy—you may be honored with a visit from some law enforcement officials.

Biodiesel, when made following the most common procedures, is safe to drink. It smells and tastes terrible and will probably give you serious intestinal cramps, but it won't have any long-term effects, unlike the diesel from the fueling station on the nearby interstate. Don't take a swig of that stuff.

Is making biodiesel worth the cost and labor? Perhaps. If you look at it as a hobby that results in paying far less cash per gallon of fuel than you would if you bought a gallon of diesel oil for your car or heating system, then your efforts will be acceptable.[58]

Biodiesel is becoming commercially available. From what I have seen, however, what's available is not pure biodiesel. It's a blend of diesel and biodiesel and will harm the environment if it is spilled.

Ethanol

The idea of powering cars with ethanol is not new. While I

---

58   https://afdc.energy.gov/files/pdfs/30882.pdf

have found no proof that the Model T was designed to be run on ethanol, it has been talked about as a fuel for automobiles through the decades. President George W. Bush was among the most recent U.S. presidents pushing for its application.

Engines and fuel systems can be designed to run on ethanol. In fact, some vehicles on the market come from the factory ready to run both gasoline and E85, a blend of 15 percent gasoline and 85 percent ethanol. So why don't we use a carbon-neutral fuel like ethanol? Well, because there are as many cons to it as there are pros.

When looking into different fuels, the concept of energy return on energy invested must be considered.[59] It's a simple concept with complex calculations that determines the amount of energy you have to invest relative to the energy returned by a given fuel. Ethanol requires a lot of energy to gain a little more energy. The actual amount depends on the sources you consult. Creating ethanol requires feedstocks with a high carbohydrate concentration such as corn, saw grass, sugar cane, and others. Making ethanol with these crops is relatively easy. Add stock, water, and yeast, allow it to ferment, distill the resulting liquid, and you have a fuel. If this sounds similar to that beverage you created in summer camp, you're right. Ethanol is that simple to make. It's just difficult economically to produce enough of a volume where it can be seriously considered as an alternative to gasoline.

The process of producing ethanol is also fraught with government red tape, whether it's used as a beverage or a fuel. There are some methods that use plants with a high cellulose content, woodchips, leaves, or similar, but those are bit more complex. Producing ethanol, whether as a beverage, fuel,

---

59   https://en.wikipedia.org/wiki/Energy_returned_on_energy_invested

or some other industrial purpose, requires federal permits and additional taxes whether or not you plan on selling it afterward.

Critics of ethanol point to its problems in spite of its near carbon neutrality: Acres of forest are being leveled to grow cane, corn, and saw grass to be used as fuel instead of for food.

Regardless of these objections, there is some hope for ethanol as an economical fuel. Research is ongoing that is investigating the use of algae and other genetically modified microorganisms to produce alcohol and biodiesel directly in a near carbon-neutral equation. These experiments have yet to scale up economically to compete with an oil field and refinery on energy produced versus that invested—but the work continues.

Hydrogen

Discussion of hydrogen as a motor fuel seems to happen sporadically. For decades it has, on occasion, been discussed for use in cars instead of gasoline.

Hydrogen releases energy as it combines with oxygen from the atmosphere and a spark. The results will be explosive energy powering the engine—much like gasoline provides—and exhaust in the form of water vapor. What could be simpler and cleaner?

The working concept in the 1970s was simply to replace the gasoline fuel system in an internal combustion engine with one that would handle gas under pressure. A simple concept, but it just didn't catch on with the general public. And once gasoline supplies became more stable, there was little interest in pursuing this concept further.

The current thinking for the use of hydrogen doesn't center on internal combustion but rather on making use of fuel cells, a technology developed by NASA decades ago to provide electrical power to manned spacecraft in the Gemini program and later the Apollo program. Fuel cells have been adapted for use on Earth. The concept behind fuel cells is to use hydrogen and ambient air passed through a catalytic filter, which results in the creation of water vapor and electricity. There is no explosion, just electricity to drive the motor (or motors) of an electric vehicle.

Some have questioned reliability of fuel cells, but I don't think that's an issue. The technology was proven though hundreds of hours under the toughest known conditions: Earth orbit and lunar voyages. In space they have the burden of having to carry extra oxygen in addition to the hydrogen.

A lot of large manufacturers have invested heavily in fuel cell technology. GM even has a novel design for a platform upon which a variety vehicle, suitable for different tasks, could be built. Plans are in place for hydrogen fuel cell trucks. Hyundai was one of the first to mass-market a fuel cell vehicle.

Although it has been eclipsed by electric cars with batteries, there was talk of a hydrogen economy. This was seen a clean counterproposal to the petroleum economy that dominates the world.

Several forms of hydrogen storage have been discussed as well, but all are experimental. The most likely form of hydrogen in a vehicle will be a contained amount of compressed hydrogen.

One of the problems with introducing an alternative fuel that may be regarded as exotic, for lack of a better term, is that there is no delivery infrastructure. Not far from where I live is a gas station that shares a parking lot with a supermarket. Off in a corner of the lot is another refueling station offering hydrogen. As of this writing, it is the only hydrogen station in Massachusetts. There are none in Rhode Island or New Hampshire.[60]

If you live close to a hydrogen refueling station, you might consider a hydrogen-powered car. I think it will be a while before the infrastructure is in place to support wide-scale use of hydrogen as a fuel, however. To use a cliché, it's a chicken/egg quandary: Consumers won't buy a hydrogen-powered vehicle if there is no convenient way to fuel it, and no corporation is going to want to build an infrastructure if the customers aren't yet there.

As I mentioned earlier, the exhaust of a hydrogen-powered vehicle would essentially be water vapor. It's nice and clean. The downside is that most hydrogen is created by reforming natural gas, or methane. The carbon and oxygen atoms are stripped from natural gas and combine to form carbon dioxide.[61] If your goal in using a hydrogen car is to reduce your carbon production, you may not be accomplishing that goal.

Not all the news about hydrogen is negative. Reforming natural gas is not the only way to produce hydrogen. One method of obtaining hydrogen is electrolysis (the separation of water atoms into hydrogen and oxygen). It's a simple process of placing a node and anode in water and capturing the released gasses. Obviously, this costs electricity, but

---

60   You can look in your area for hydrogen or other alternative fuel stations on this Department of Energy website: https://afdc.energy.gov/stations/#/find/nearest

61   https://hydrogeneurope.eu/hydrogen-production-0

surplus electric capacity during off-peak usage hours could be used to harvest hydrogen from water for use as a motor fuel.

The electric car

Electric cars are nothing new. At the dawn of the twentieth century the internal combustion engine was not the only option when considering personal transportation. There was also the famous Stanley Steamer, a contemporary of the Ford Model T. According to some historians, electric cars were once the market leader. They were quieter than gasoline and didn't require a hand crank to start. Neither did they require a warm-up like steam; they just moved when you turned on the switch. And considering people didn't make many long-distance trips and roads were usually only paved in the city at the time, you were probably not far from home when the battery started running low.

Even though the nation's electrical infrastructure was also in its infancy, the electric car was a market leader.[62] Even a subsidiary of General Electric was involved by way of a battery exchange. Similar to many services offered today, when your battery was getting low you could drive to a service center and have it swapped out for a fresh battery.

The modern electric car is in a completely different world. Electricity reaches even the most remote parts of North America. Because of laws enacted as far back as the 1930s, like the Rural Electrification Act that helped build the national infrastructure, very few people wonder where you would plug in an electric car.

---

62   https://www.energy.gov/timeline/timeline-history-electric-car

What is hampering modern electric cars is the same thing that hampered the older models about a century ago: Battery life is limited, and recharging or swapping takes time. On the other hand filling up on gasoline was, and still is, a quick errand on the way home.

Modern technology and a bit of ingenuity have improved things a bit. Today's electrics are sleek and aerodynamic, minimizing the energy required to push through the air. Internet searches make it easier to locate charging stations at, or conveniently near, our destinations. Whereas a hydrogen-powered car owner may have difficulty locating fuel when a hundred miles from home, an electric car owner can probably find a compatible charging station and "tank up" while shopping, eating at a restaurant, or staying over at a hotel. Many such businesses make a point of advertising their charging stations. It's not too expensive to install a charger at one's home, either.[63]

With increased efficiency in battery life and enhancements to the existing electrical infrastructure, electric cars are coming quickly—and not just from niche manufacturers like Tesla but from established motor industry giants like Volkswagen, GM, Freightliner, and Ford.

Of course, there are the detractors who will remind us that the electricity in an electric car's battery was derived from a relatively dirty, fossil fuel-burning source just like the fossil fuel-burning cars on the highway right now. I won't disagree. Even if you've bought carbon offsets or your utility has earned some RECs, carbon dioxide is still being

---

63   Although beyond the scope of this essay, there is talk about using your electric car as a battery backup for critical home systems in the event of a blackout. https://www.fastcompany.com/90316119/this-suv-can-power-your-house-and-your-house-can-charge-its-battery

produced somewhere. However, it is my opinion that one well maintained plant providing power to 10,000 electric vehicles is going to be less polluting and better supervised than 10,000 gasoline or diesel engines in various states of repair and mechanical condition.

What powers your next car?

While I am a firm believer in keeping options open and I see the advantages of carbon-neutral and carbon-less fuels for personal transportation, I'm also optimistic about their use in the long term. If you compare the alternative fuels to current electric car technology, there is a clear advantage to the alternative power sources. The key is refueling time. A tankful of gasoline, ethanol, diesel, or hydrogen can all be obtained in a matter of minutes. The best that current electric vehicles can do is a partial charge in thirty to forty minutes, while a full charge takes up to eight hours. (This can vary by vehicle and the voltage available.) I think this limitation will be overcome and the infrastructure improved even further so that electric vehicle will eventually represent the majority on the road.

One further note: In a very rural section of a town near the Rhode Island line, I have come across a family that has several electric and plug-in hybrid cars. They park their vehicles under a carport that has solar panels on its roof. They don't seem to pay a lot for fuel.

⁂

The "quick fix" of our motor fuel supply: A story of unintended consequences

Earlier I discussed some business practices in which people, despite good intentions and due only to ignorance or short-sightedness, introduced harm to the environment. Plastic ratification to replace wood and paper is a prime example. This issue is not related just to solid wastes, though. There have been many instances where a product was introduced to the environment to fix one problem but generated a possibly worse effect.

Such was the case of a chemical called methyltert-butylether, or MTBE. MTBE was introduced as early as the 1970s into gasoline by some manufacturers as an agent to increase octane and decrease knock in gasoline engines. It was used to replace lead in gasoline, which was considered a major victory for the environment. MTBE made engines run a little smoother and pollute a bit less. Lead had been removed from motor fuels in other states but was not necessarily replaced with gasoline containing MBTE. By the early 1990s, however, many states began to require it to be added to gasoline sold in their states in an effort to improve air quality. This included the New England states.

There were complaints—mostly from me—that the new MBTE blends were not only a little more expensive but seemed to cause a slight drop in gas mileage. (This part is anecdotal, but the story continues.)

As the months went by, areas that had no problems with groundwater were starting to have problems. Private and municipal wells were starting to show signs of pollution. MBTE, it turns, out travels very quickly through groundwater.

The taste of our water was affected, and the problems went further…

Finally, people—i.e., the relevant government agency—realized that the goal of cleaner air resulted in increased water pollution.

The usual lawsuits were filed. Some of the chemical companies that were selling MBTE paid fines for improper handling of the chemicals. Eventually the rules changed and MBTE was replaced with ethanol. The producers of ethanol were happy, at least. The towns and individuals that had their water supplies contaminated spent billions to clean them up.[64]

The moral of this tale: All potential consequences must be taken into consideration when implementing large-scale changes like tinkering with the public motor fuel supply.

---

64   https://www.bostonglobe.com/metro/2012/11/09/two-oil-companies-pay-mtbe-suit/as3lZa2s0yfZA0t8mWbLKJ/story.html

OTHER TRANSPORTATION SYSTEMS

Ground transportation: What we do wrong[65]

This section is grounded in the Boston, MA area but the thoughts are easily applicable to other regions of the country.

The majority of the Massachusetts population live within thirty miles of Boston, a city ringed by two major highways and serviced by a mediocre commuter rail system and failing subway system. The inner ring road, locally referred to as Route 128, is officially designated in some sections as Interstate Highways 95 and 93 (that's a long story).

Although Boston boasts the oldest subway system in America, built in the nineteenth century, the majority of the state's transportation budget since the 1950s has been spent on highways, bridges, and tunnels for motor vehicle traffic.

---

65   Many thanks to Lisa M. Grasso for her contribution to this section of the book.

Billions of taxpayer dollars have been spent on projects with the goal of moving cars, trucks, and busses efficiently from one part of the state to another. One project which became nationally known as "The Big Dig" was intended to replace an obsolete stretch of highway in downtown Boston with a wider underground highway. In a phenomenon known as "project creep," rolled into the project were some new bridges and ancillary tunnels, new ramps, and rerouted utilities. The tunnels went under and above subways and railroad tracks. It was a true marvel of engineering and logistics. All of this work was done with minimal interruption of highway and public transportation traffic. ("Minimal," being a relative concept, will be debated for some time.)

The final cost, excluding ongoing maintenance, was 22.8 billion dollars, nearly eight times the original estimate. To be fair, a number of projects were added onto the original proposal that greatly increased the cost. In order to help pay for the Big Dig, maintenance and new road projects throughout the state were cut back or eliminated.

The result was, it didn't help. Traffic is just as bad as ever. Rush hour in Boston and the surrounding cities out to the suburbs is an all-day affair. Had the number of cars on the road not increased as the years went by, the project may have been an improvement in traffic flow. Who knows?

Unfortunately for the highway planners, the population in the region increased. Colleges and universities continued to expand and more businesses popped up. Jobs were created as tech companies prospered further away from the city along Route 128 and even out to the outer belt of Interstate 495. The old situation of most people living in the suburbs and commuting to downtown Boston shifted. Highways are not adaptable to changed traffic flows, and mass transit serving suburb-to-suburb commuting barely exists. More vehicles stuck in traffic means more air pollution, wasted time, and wasted gasoline.

The neglect of other transportation projects while the Big Dig was sucking up all the funding left the remainder of eastern Massachusetts with less serviceable roads and a public transit system that is mediocre at best, an embarrassment at worst.

In Boston and the immediate suburbs, the subways, trolleys, and light rail still run on tracks in need of repair. Extensions of transit lines are far behind schedule. Every public transit commuter will tell you a nightmare commute story about breakdowns, missed runs, and derailments occurring at near third-world frequency.

As a result of poorly planned capacity of the road system and the neglect of the public transit system, commuters are left with few options besides to expect delays and have their patience tested.

A poor transit system has economic implications. Companies will have trouble attracting employees and moving goods and materials efficiently. Residents will become discouraged and start looking for homes in towns more convenient to their jobs or for jobs in areas with better transit options.

Unless comprehensive planning and programs are put into place, the quality of life and the environment will steadily decline. Having neglected public transit, more and more people are being forced into their cars, most of which still require gasoline or diesel fuel.

Many Massachusetts workers actually reside in nearby Rhode Island and New Hampshire. Although getting multiple independently elected governments to work together on transportation plans adds levels of complexity, it does not mean that all is lost. There are some ideas out there to mitigate the transportation problem and the pollution that accompanies an inefficient system. One idea is a proposal called the Transportation and Climate Initiative (TCI).[66]

I'm a big proponent of regional cooperation. In Massachusetts, as in other states, we have authorities that handle services that extend beyond the individual. MassPort handles state airports and seaports; the MBTA1 handles public transportation in the eastern part of the state.

The TCI is a regional compact between many of the northeastern states and several others as far south as Virginia, and that also includes Washington, D.C. The goal of the TCI is to have the twelve states (and D.C.) in which it has been proposed working together to make up for the failings of the federal government and to push for higher standards when it comes to reducing pollution.[67]

Unfortunately, the wording of the act and its purpose is light on details about funding formulae and the amount of control each state will have. Will representation be pro rata—with New York, Pennsylvania, and Virginia controlling most of the money—or will it be an organization of equals—where Rhode Island, Delaware, and D.C. are on equal footing with New York?

A big political sticking point is a provision proposed to enact fees on sellers of carbon fuels, which are tantamount to taxes not voted on by a legislature. The proponents of the

---

66   https://www.mass.gov/info-details/transportation-and-climate-initiative-tci

67   https://blog.ucsusa.org/daniel-gatti/the-transportation-and-climate-initiative-explained

TCI say the money collected would go to transportation and clean energy projects. There are few details written into the act about how exactly the funds would be distributed and which future projects would be funded.

The Massachusetts legislature has a poor record of following through on spending earmarked money for its intended purpose. In the early 1990s a ballot referendum was passed by the voters to significantly raise the gasoline tax. I voted in favor. The referendum's proponents said the money collected would go to fix bridges and roads throughout the commonwealth. Very few infrastructure projects benefited from the tax, however. The legislature was not obligated to spend that money on infrastructure and most of the money that did reach road projects went specifically toward the Big Dig.

No one wants to see a repeat of that.

Another concern is that rural and ex-urban residents, who have few options for transportation besides private vehicles, will benefit the least. There is nothing to prevent the fees collected through the TCI from benefitting urban area projects only and ignoring those outside of the cities.

Because rural people tend to spend more per capita on gasoline and diesel and they earn a lower income per person than their urban counterparts, fuel taxes are inherently regressive and the fees collected by the TCI would not prove of much benefit without strict oversight of how the money is distributed and how the organization is supervised.

I favor regional cooperation to solve problems, but I also favor strong oversight of this cooperation.

Ground transportation: What we can do right

Massachusetts, like many other states, has concentrated too many resources in the past decades on one unsustainable transportation system. For many people, myself included, the one transportation option is single occupancy of a gasoline-powered vehicle.

We created a system that people have little choice but to use if they need to get around the region. Switching to public transit may not be practical; if even ten percent of the people in low-occupied vehicles tried to take the MBTA[68] subways and busses, the public transportation system would be quickly overwhelmed.

This may sound like an anti-big-government rant, but one can truly say that our elected officials lack awareness and imagination when it comes to certain programs—and transportation is one of them. We need big ideas and a long-term-thinking politician willing to see those ideas through. Failure to do so will only stifle future growth in both business and recreation.

Several years ago, a group of business and political leaders got together to draft a proposal to bring the 2024 Olympics to Boston. The idea was met with strong resistance. The most cited reason why Boston should not bid on the Olympics was: "The region can't handle the traffic." Not, "the region can't handle the influx of people." Just the *traffic*. The wording indicates that the only considerable means of transportation were the roads.

A couple of years after the idea of an Olympic bid was dropped the Boston area, along with many other cities around

68   A lesson in Bay State linguistics. The MBTA refers to the overall transportation authority, including subways, busses, trolleys, and commuter rail. However when someone in Massachusetts says they are "taking the T," they are referring to one of the subways or surface light rail trains.

the country, tried to convince technology giant Amazon to locate a second headquarters in the city. Amazon would bring tens of thousands of jobs and pump billions into the economy. Again, the naysayers were wringing their hands over the traffic. Automobiles. No thought was given to potential improvement in subways, the light rail, the commuter rail, or the installation of dedicated pedestrian and bike routes. All improvements that could have been built with anticipated tax revenue as the Amazon jobs started to roll in. We just worried about the traffic.

Boston lost that bid to other regions, yet we did not learn our lesson. Local politicians tried to put a positive spin on it by claiming we dodged a bullet. Unless we get serious about developing a multi-mode transportation system, Boston and eastern New England are destined to become economic backwaters.

Big ideas, big transportation

At home and in my professional life I try to go by the guidelines of positive thinking. One of those guidelines is: If you are going to complain, also try to come up with a solution—even if it seems far-fetched. It may get others thinking. Here's one of my complaints:

Many elected officials and appointed government employees don't realize that the economy is a seven-days-a-week, twenty-four-hours-a-day enterprise. While Boston is still central to the region's financial, cultural, and educational spheres, it is not the only place where activity happens. As mentioned previously, the bulk of highway and mass transit in Massachusetts has been built under the assumption that people are heading into Boston to get to work by nine and then leaving for home at five. Sometime in the 1980s, that arrangement began to change. Office parks grew in the suburbs, first in the towns along Route 128 and then beyond, to the areas further out than Interstate 495. There were no comprehensive transportation plans to reflect what may be the bulk of commuting in the commonwealth, from Worcester to the North and South Shores. Many people no longer exclusively commute from a suburb into Boston; they commute from one suburb to another, for which there are no practical mass transit options.

I'm sure I'm not the first person to sit in stopped traffic on one of the region's major roads and look at that wide, barely used median strip and wonder why it isn't used for something like a light rail line that would serve the outer suburbs. Maybe even electric trolleys at the major interchanges and shuttle services at the minor ones. If not light rail, then maybe separate bus lanes in the median—but still have the shuttles at the interchanges (using electric busses). And don't forget bicycle lanes as another option from the interchanges to people's destinations.

With so many technical improvements, much of the system could be composed of self-driving vehicles. The issue of having to pay employees a premium to work after certain hours, on weekends, or holidays would be eliminated.

If this were implemented and a reasonable fare was charged, you would get a lot of people out of their cars and onto public transportation. With modern tech, it would be easy to track ride distance and charge by the mile.

Will my brilliant plan ever be instituted? Maybe not, but it's an example to point out the benefits of starting with a clean slate. In a state where more was spent on one highway project than was spent in the previous thirty years (even after adjusting for inflation), then maybe the approach should be not to rebuild but to replace large sections of the state's infrastructure.

I'm not alone in my tendency to place blame on elected officials and their appointed agency heads. But those of us who are not politicians or state employees also have to take part of the blame. We elected them. If you want action, then support candidates who can support big ideas. Six decades ago it was a Bay State politician who said we would put a man on the moon by the end of the decade (i.e., before 1970). Many of the researchers, scientists, engineers, and factory workers who made it possible were also from Massachusetts. Working together, I'm sure we can come up with a way to get people to work on time.

Ground transportation: A quick rant

Another quirk about Boston transportation is its two main railroad terminals, located about five miles apart with no direct link between the two. North Station and South Station are their names. Back when rail was the main form of long-distance travel, trains from Maine, New Hampshire, and Vermont would be served by North Station while trains from points south and west of Boston went into South Station. Passengers would have to find alternate transportation between the two if they were to continue past Boston. Until the 1970s there was an indirect link with freight lines running from both stations to the seaport area, but these trains did not transfer passengers.

The two terminal locations are still there. They have seen some changes over the decades, but there is still no link between the two. People traveling from the south of Boston wanting to get transportation north have to switch to subways with a change between lines, walk, or take a car or bus.

It's not for lack of interest. Over the years there have been many proposals for links between the two. There is a cycle that has been on repeat for as long as I can remember: Transportation officials recognize the need for a link, proposals are sought, proposals are reviewed, the legislature debates, the legislature gets distracted by other priorities, the idea is shelved. In a few years someone else will notice the need for a link.

The cycle may end someday. There are a couple of proposals being considered. There are two factors that won't change in all of this: The need will not go away and the cost will not go down.

Government organizations: Another quick rant

We need to make sure that our government agencies are staying true to their missions. Citizens' demands that money collected via taxes and mass transit fares go to pay for the actual purpose of the agencies. Like many bureaucracies, transportation departments tend to lose sight of their purpose. Lax oversight results in the waste of taxpayers' money and the perception that people don't like to take public transportation.

The opposite of that perception is true. In many areas, given a practical alternative, many people would take clean and reliable public transportation.[69] In many parts of the country people are driving less and taking buses and light rail when practical.

⫻

High-speed rail: What's all the fuss

If you want to split into factions at a neighborhood cookout, bring up the idea of high-speed rail travel. Okay, maybe factions will only form if the cookout is a gathering of a bunch of political nerds… but it's still fun to discuss.

I have traveled to several different countries on business and personal trips over the years. In many countries outside the United States, public rail systems are an integral part of daily life in metropolitan areas, and not just for people who hop onto light rail or commuter trains to get to work or students going to class via subway (or metro, or whatever it might be called where you live). In many countries a long-distance, efficient, high-speed rail is just another part of the mix. For instance, Japan, France, and Norway incorporate an efficient rail system that offer a practical alternative to air travel for relatively short trips of a few hundred miles or less.

On our first trip to Japan more than ten years ago, my wife and I tried to do our best not to stick out. Okay, as two slightly taller than average Americans, we were conspicuous

---

69   https://www.wsj.com/articles/americas-love-affair-with-driving-takes-a-back-seat-11577183402?emailToken=12f0b da053f62d471d142417fedab961vQDNp3NGcWLD+tG1zQEaz 6YoR6FJvacaDnCHXyAtIJc68v1fGE7pe2jUoJFgPTiXmwWdL/ WWx9OzUuspaHotfDd3sxAP1frWn+ZaDhcArPQ%3D&reflink=article_ copyURL_share

while walking through Shibuya, but that didn't mean we couldn't experience modern Japanese life.

Our host and hostess for that trip were a younger brother and his extremely patient wife who are great at making their guests feel welcome. They helped us purchase our subway passes and find maps and guides in English so we could get around like everyone else in the area and not have to pay a fortune for taxis—that is, if the drivers even spoke enough English to understand where we wanted to go.

On that trip my brother mentioned that he had to take an overnight business trip to Hiroshima. He would be flying out the night before his meeting, but he suggested we take the bullet train and join him later the next day for a tour of the area, and then he would accompany us on the train back to Tokyo.

Looking at a map we could see that from where we were staying in the Tokyo prefecture it was more than four hundred miles to Hiroshima station. The Bullet Train, or Shinkansen, as it's officially known in Japan, makes the trip in about four hours, including the time it takes to get to the station and change trains in Osaka. My sister-in-law gave us explicit instructions and had enough confidence in us that she didn't pin notes to our coats with the name and number of whom to call in case we got lost.

I was still having trouble believing the estimated travel time of four hours. In the U.S., four hours is barely time to drive to an airport, check in, go through security… you get the drill. And we would be dropped right in the middle of Hiroshima.

The Shinkansen was quieter than an airliner and traveled at speeds of close to 200 miles per hour. The cars are pressurized so you don't get the noise and compression feeling when a train goes under a bridge or into a tunnel with low clearance.

We don't have such a service in this country; we rely on air travel instead. The last major airport built from the ground up was Denver's 4.5-billion-dollar airport, which was completed more than twenty years ago. Even though there are no new major airports being built, we continue to spend billions of dollars annually upgrading and renovating existing facilities.

It occurred to me on a recent trip to Seattle, Washington that I have never been in a finished airport. It seems as soon as an airport is complete it has to be expanded or have runways added or terminals and traffic patterns reconfigured.

Banning air travel would be extremely impractical; no one in today's economy has the time to take days to cross the country by rail (unless that trans-continental American bullet train comes through) or an ocean by ship. But the thought occurred to me while flying to the Detroit area: rather than grabbing a local train and then a high-speed rail to go the eight hundred or so miles to Detroit in comfort, I drove to an airport, parked and waited for a shuttle, made sure I was there an hour early to catch my flight, went through security, and waited to board. Maybe even a bullet train ride from Boston to Detroit might be a bit long for a business trip, but what if we had high-speed rail to replace connecting flights? I've traveled many times to Newark, New Jersey, or Philadelphia to catch a flight to Europe or the mid-east. If I could have taken a high-speed train from Providence to one of those cities, then I could have avoided the airport "experience" in Providence and only had to deal with one airport.

As anyone who has had to change planes for a connecting flight on the way home from a foreign country will appreciate, it would mean one less trip through security.

A new rail system would be expensive... but what does an airport cost?

At the risk of repeating myself—airports cost a lot of money to build and maintain and are often obsolete as soon as they're finished. When was the last time you went through a major airport and saw no construction-related activity? I don't ever remember that happening even at the relatively small Green Airport in Rhode Island.

The infrastructure to support an airport is enormous. Jet fuel is brought via pipelines from depots or ports far away from the airport itself. Highways and bridges are often required or at least get included with major renovations, increased security, and the inevitable lawsuits by the abutters and even people miles away trying to get airport noise mitigated.

Some people find train travel more convenient than airplanes. Since the attacks of September 11, 2001, many people in the Northeast stick to ground transportation when traveling between New York City, Philadelphia, Boston, and Providence. Travelers have realized that skipping airport security and traveling from downtown terminal to downtown terminal makes spending an extra couple of hours relaxing or working on your laptop worth it.

If trips of six or seven hundred miles by train were convenient and speedy, we could save a lot of money and personal stress as well as ease the effects on the environment with a high-speed rail system—especially in the congested urban areas that continue to become more congested.

The building of such a system would pump billions of dollars into the economy which, as any Intro to Economics student knows, will have a multiplying effect as more jobs are created, companies are formed to support the rails system, and other companies form to supply the needs of the people paid for the work on and around the lines.

Airlines aren't going to disappear; they will just be able to concentrate on the longer, more profitable long-haul flights.

Certain types of freight transportation could probably benefit by faster rail. Although I haven't been able to find much information on mail or light freight hauled on high-speed trains, there's no reason a car or two couldn't be added for that purpose. This would include fresh fruit and vegetables shipped even faster without the added environmental overhead of freight aircraft.

I could go on for another five thousand words on high-speed rail versus short-haul air travel, but that would just belabor the point. If you want to see firsthand how a high-speed rail system can make travel easier, I recommend visiting a country where it is in use. Try it out. You will be convinced.

A quick word on the facilities on the Shinkansen: If you need to use a lavatory, read the signs carefully. They won't say *Men* and *Women*, they will say *Western toilet* and *Japanese toilet*. You want to use the former unless you're seeking a fully immersive cultural experience.

⚏

Air travel and ecotourism: A paradox in the making?

Sustainable tourism and ecotourism are terms that have been appearing recently in newspaper and magazine tourism sections. Sometimes they are used interchangeably, but they are not really synonymous.

"Sustainable tourism" refers to taking measures to mitigate the effect your travels have had on the economy. This can look like do-it-yourself purchases of carbon offsets to make up for the fuel you've burned, be it via airplane, cruise ship, diesel train, or a drive in your own car to see Aunt Millie on her farm over in Quabbin. It can mean booking your travel, hotels, and activities through an agency that can provide proof of carbon mitigation through reputable and certified organizations.

Ecotourism is the practice of traveling to threatened or fragile areas to observe these areas and help impress upon yourself and your family the importance of saving these areas from destruction through neglect, development, or climate changes. I know people who have traveled to South American rain forests, Asian jungles, and Antarctic glacier fields. Ecotourism offers benefits beyond providing yourself concrete proof that these areas exist and should be protected. If done right, you can help support some of the organizations that aim to save these areas.

But there is a paradox to ecotourism, even if you are very careful and do your best to neutralize the effects of your visit. Your firsthand testimony can spread the word that these places need protecting. What happens when everyone gets word of the existence of a beautiful and fragile place in need of protection? I suppose that question is rhetorical. There is the risk of the number of visitors increasing to beyond the point of sustainability.

In a previous section I brought up the game theory concept of the "Tragedy of the Commons," where a self-replenishing resource gradually reaches the limit of how much it can take before it becomes diminished beyond recovery.[70]

Perhaps you want to visit an old growth forest. There are several such sites in Massachusetts alone.[71] If care isn't taken, too many people trampling already well-worn paths can affect the movement of water and small animals that are vital to the way a forest maintains itself. Perhaps someone might see lady slipper, one of the few orchids native to the Northeast, and not be able to resist touching it. Such visits can have a negative effect on the fragile ecosystem.

If such a thing could happen to what we see as hardy woodlands of New England, what would happen to a rainforest or jungle if too many people were to move through or if an airport nearby needed to be expanded due to the influx of visitors?

When I read about people visiting unusual places, I think of the photos I've seen of the lines of people climbing Mount Everest. As a child I always imagined an Everest climb as experience where every year a few teams of expert mountaineers and their experienced guides fight the elements and the mountain itself to achieve the summit. The only other human contact might be another party in the distance.

The recent news photos and videos of Everest during prime climbing season paint a different picture, however. The

---

70   https://phys.org/news/2020-02-tourists-pose-disease-transmission-endangered.html

71   https://www.massaudubon.org/our-conservation-work/advocacy/protecting-land-wildlife/forest-policy/old-growth

teams heading toward the summit form what looks like a vertical conga line.

The government of Tibet limits the number of climbing permits it issues each year. The government of Nepal, which controls other parts of the mountain does not limit the permits issued, however. Pretty much anyone who can come up with the $11,000 fee will be issued a permit. Economics plays a big factor, but how long will it be before Everest is too crowded and the environment around base camps is so damaged that people start to think that the *I climbed Mount Everest* T-shirts aren't worth it?

Our best hope is that the governments that control such interesting, yet fragile, areas will do their best to calculate the number of visitors that an area can safely accommodate without destroying a valuable natural and economic resource.

I won't tell people where to go or how to spend their money. One can only hope that, when booking a trip to a fragile, protected area, people consider what they can do to mitigate their environmental impact to the region they plan to visit.

If you want to help mitigate what you feel to be your effect on the environment when you travel, look into supporting an organization such as The Good Traveler, whose website contains a lot of information on how you can do your part to lessen your travels' effects on the environment.[72]

---

72   https://thegoodtraveler.org/

A second look at the modern skyscraper

Nearly every major American city has at least one landmark building that practically represents it. New York City has the Chrysler Building and the Empire State Building. Boston has the Prudential Building. Detroit, Chicago, Los Angeles, even Providence, Rhode Island have their showpiece buildings. Steel and concrete behemoth skyscrapers have come to define the skylines of modern metropolises around the globe since the early twentieth century.

Is there another way to build cities? Does every large building have to be steel skeletons, concrete floors, and curtain-hung panels? What if they were not made of steel and concrete but of wood? In that case they wouldn't be thirty story tall cottages but structures specially designed to take advantage of one of man's oldest building materials.

Architects and builders are looking into various engineered materials that are based on wood. These engineered materials are showing similar strength to weight ratios as steel and concrete. There are several factors that are leading to the acceptance of wood—or should I say, *re-acceptance* of wood— as a material for large structures.

"Mass timber construction" is the term used for building with these new materials and techniques. The material may consist of large sawn pieces of timber or smaller pieces glued together into supporting beams and solid panels. The panels differ from plywood in that plywood is composed of thin layers (plies) of wood held together by glue.[73] Plywood is not as flame retardant as are the mass timber engineered pieces. While the latter are obviously not as flame resistant

---

73   https://www.constructiondive.com/news/mass-timber-101-understanding-the-emerging-building-type/443476/

as steel and concrete, extra measures can be taken to guard against fire, such as adding more sprinkler heads and covering exposed wood, except as architecturally desirable. Mass timber construction exceeds the flame resistance requirements of most building codes.[74]

The unavoidable question is, why replace the tried-and-true steel and concrete method of building a high-rise with what seems like a regressive method?

Let's start with the basics. Concrete is rough on the environment. Making it requires mining the basic limestone, grinding, exposing it to extreme heat, transporting it to where it's to be used, mixing it with water and other material, then pouring it into place. Steel is also a resource hog from the mining and transportation of iron ore to the rolling and milling into columns, beams, and trusses, transportation to the site, and welding into place.

Wood, on the other hand, requires a lot less to harvest, prepare, and make ready as a useful material.[75] Add to that the fact that wood is naturally carbon sequestering. (If the carbon is in the wood, it's not in the atmosphere.)

Wood is, as a construction material, renewable. If you read the section on energy, you may think I'm contradicting myself, but I am not. Wood as a fuel is considered by many agencies as non-renewable because it may take twenty to twenty-five years to grow a cord of hardwood such as oak or maple that will provide heating for a small home for a couple of months. Then it will take another twenty years, at least, to replace that cord.

---

74   https://www.thinkwood.com/news/4-things-to-know-about-mass-timber

75   https://www.thinkwood.com/news/4-things-to-know-about-mass-timber

Wood in construction lasts indefinitely; but let's consider the life of a building to be the length of time over which the Internal Revenue Service allows building owners to amortize their property. Currently the law allows amortization over twenty-seven to thirty-nine years, depending on the purpose of the building.[76] During that time, the forest can replace much of the wood that was harvested for the building that was erected.

Wood will not replace concrete and steel everywhere, of course. The George Washington Bridge could not have been built from wood, nor could the Empire State Building. That doesn't mean that many smaller bridges couldn't be built from mass timber construction, especially in colder areas of the country where road salt rots out steel and damages steel-reinforced concrete.[77]

There are other alternatives that may offer the best of both worlds—the strength of concrete and the carbon sequestering of wood.[78]

It will a take a lot of convincing to get real estate developers, architects, and civil engineers to look away from steel and concrete buildings and bridges and look toward adding renewable wood into the mix.

---

76   https://www.irs.gov/pub/irs-pdf/f4562.pdf (My intent is not to give tax advice. Consult your tax professional.)

77   https://www.nordic.ca/en/projects/mass-timber-bridges (The Nordic Structures website also shows some beautiful bridge designs of which wood is one of the primary materials.)

78   https://apple.news/AClB5Wjy0Sb24r7Ho3M2GSQ

It's time we get honest about our gadgets

In my profession, technical change is inevitable. It's a cliché to write that over the past thirty years the pace of change in technology has been accelerating exponentially. My job is essential to support the enterprise-level use of technology that didn't exist ten years ago and may be considered obsolete in another ten.

At one time, technology seemed permanent. If your great-grandfather bought an AM/shortwave radio back in the 1930s and it was maintained, it will still receive AM and shortwave broadcasts. If Grandpa bought an FM radio in the 1960s, that radio still receives broadcasts too. (I will reserve comment on the quality of the content). These devices are not obsolete because they still perform a useful function and are supported in the market. Of course there are some better radios on the market now, as well as alternatives to radio, but that doesn't mean you can't turn on the shortwave, warm it up, and listen to broadcasts from around the world.

When my parents bought a TV in the 1980s, no one except for some engineers foresaw the switch to digital television. Yet, in 2009, just a short while back, analog television receivers were rendered obsolete by the Federal Communication Commission. They mandated the switch to all digital television in order that they could eliminate analog television broadcasts. Low-cost devices that attached to an analog television's antenna connections were offered to convert the digital signal to analog, so people did not have to get rid of their analog receivers—but not as many people bought the converters as forecast. Instead, digital high-definition televisions experienced such a dramatic drop in price, as often happens with technology, that people went digital. (There are still some low-power television broadcasters using analog signals but not many companies offer analog receivers.)

When the switch came, millions of televisions then headed to the basement, the attic, landfill, or (hopefully) recycling, joining the Betamax video cassette recorders and eight-track tape players. I refer to VCRs and eight-track players as obsolete because it is getting difficult to find blank media for either one and no company is mass-producing prerecorded tapes. Turntables would be on the list, but they are enjoying a Renaissance. Aficionados of vinyl records have increased to such a level that classic long-playing albums (LPs) are being re-released and many artists are releasing new material on vinyl as well as compact disc and streaming services.

That's why it's important that, with few exceptions, we stop thinking of our electronic gadgets as permanent purchases and realize that most of them will be replaced before they actually have to be due to wear and tear. Compare your current smartphone to an analog cell phone of the nineties.

Some products are declared obsolete simply because, although they are still functional, we want to replace them with a device that has more or better features. Because of this idea of obsolescence before expiration, it is important to look carefully at what you buy. Be honest with yourself and realize that cell phone or television will not be the last one you ever buy. Consider your purchases with more than an eye on price and features. Go online and research the percentage of recycled materials that go into your new phone of computer and the recyclability of the virgin materials. Some manufacturers use a lot more recyclable content in their devices than others.

Earlier in this book I discussed the content in Dell and Apple computers. Hold other manufacturers to the same standard.

Another thing to keep in mind is the proper disposal of the technological devices you already own (see Appendix D regarding their disposal).

The Environmental Protection Agency

Why are we gutting the EPA?

Political parties tend to revel in the positive aspects of their histories.

Democrats are quick to point out FDR and the New Deal and the winning of WWII. They boast of the brief Camelot era when it seemed the U.S. could do anything, including starting a formal manned space program with the goal of landing astronauts on the moon and returning them safely home.

The Republicans have their highlights, too. They like to remind others that Lincoln was the one who kept the country together and ended slavery. How Teddy Roosevelt turned the country into a world power, built a canal, and came up with programs that helped business to flourish while ending monopolies. He also made the National Parks an official part of the U.S. government—going far beyond the haphazard protections that dated back to when Lincoln secured the area around Yosemite. But during all the celebration of the accomplishments of the Republican Party, there is one administration that is often left off the list: that of Richard M. Nixon.

The Nixon era is best known for some really bad events in our history as well as some really amazing ones. Obviously, there is the Watergate scandal, the pending impeachment, and the ultimate resignation in disgrace of the president. Then, for the first time in our nation's history, the head of the executive branch was somebody who wasn't elected. There was also the de-escalation of the Vietnam War where most combat troops were brought back home and, of course, the successful landing of men on the moon and their safe return.

I will not deny the corrupt political practices of Nixon and his associates but there is one historic event that isn't usually associated with his administration: the formation of the Environmental Protection Agency.

In 1970, Nixon signed into law the creation of an independent and powerful agency within the government whose sole purpose was to protect the environment from threats related to human activity. The EPA is considered so important that its head, while not a cabinet-level officer, is often treated as such by the president and those holding cabinet positions.

Many actions of the EPA have been and continue to be controversial, but its success cannot be denied. Coordination of lawsuits, grants, and state cooperation have made two of Boston's most historic bodies of water clean enough for recreation and, on occasion, swimming. Boston Harbor and the Charles River, which runs from Hopkinton, Massachusetts to the harbor, were once seen as open sewers. Little effort was made to stop the flow of sewage and toxic chemicals that were dumped in the water as a matter of course by the cities, towns, and businesses along the course. Today, thanks to the work of thousands of individuals and dozens of agencies, falling into either body of water does not earn you an automatic trip to the hospital to treat some inevitable reactions or to get a tetanus shot. There is a famous picture of then Governor William Weld celebrating the success of the cleanup by leaping from a Cambridge boat dock into the Charles River. It's not yet perfect, however.

Earlier I discussed the cleaning up of the Blackstone River watershed from Worcester to Narragansett Bay. Massachusetts and Rhode Island are not the only states with success stories like this one. Nearly every state has benefitted or is in the process of benefitting from the cleanup of some polluted land in order to make it useable for other purposes. These are known as "brownfields" in industry jargon (probably much to the chagrin of the good people of Brownfield, Maine).

Companies conforming to EPA regulations will prevent another Love Canal- or WR Grace-like incident that caused cancer, birth defects, and other forms of physical misery for decades after the original offenses were committed.

If you want another example of the effectiveness of the EPA, stand next to a classic car built in any year between the fifties and the mid-seventies. Ask the owner to start the ignition and, as you admire the deep-throated purr of a classic big-block V-8 or in-line six-cylinder engine, take a walk around to the back of the car. You will notice the smell of unburned hydrocarbons on even the most carefully preserved and tuned engine of the era. Imagine a city whose streets are filled with such cars, and you will have an idea of why cities like Los Angeles and even New York City would have regular smog alerts.

Yet, instead of praising the EPA, many of my fellow conservatives condemn it as obstructionist, an economic liability, and an agency that has outlived its usefulness.

Admittedly, sometimes the EPA has seemed to push things too far. There are stories about massive projects that had years of review and permissions behind them only to be further sidetracked from the mission because a rare or previously unknown biological specimen had been discovered. (These are anecdotes of the exceptions.)

In 2017 President Donald Trump signed an executive order (13771) that contains a lot of words to say that for every regulation a federal agency wants to put into effect, two must be revoked. Any government regulation has the potential to be difficult, and those from the EPA are no exception. But the get-one-for-two rule is an extreme and arbitrary way to get rid of them.

The EPA has become the unfortunate target of many special interest groups mostly because it is trying to balance economic growth with minimizing or completely mitigating environmental damage. Because of this, many regulations are being considered for suspension or revocation and other proposed regulations have been removed from consideration.

The *New York Times* has not been a friend of a Republican administration since Eisenhower, and even then, it wasn't all that close. The newspaper is not the neutral reporter of world events it should be. That being said, it published an article detailing a number of rules that were changed, delayed, or removed from active regulation. The analysis, based on research from Harvard Law School, Columbia Law School, and other sources, counts more than ninety environmental rules and regulations rolled back under the Trump administration.

President Trump has made eliminating federal regulations a priority. His administration, with help from Republicans in Congress, has often targeted environmental rules it sees as burdensome to the fossil fuel industry and other big businesses... Our list represents two types of policy changes: rules that were officially reversed and rollbacks still in progress.[79]

These regulations are far-ranging, from ammunition that can be used on federal land, to lands where oil and gas recovery is barred. Some may have been burdensome on the individual, but many were seen as simply political maneuvers.

The Trump administration has rolled back or is attempting to roll back regulations pertaining to air pollution and emissions, the drilling and extraction of minerals and fossil fuels, infrastructure, animal and endangered species, toxins, and water pollution. The EPA has eased restrictions on refineries and oil drillers on the amount of methane they release into the atmosphere as well as where drilling can take place.

Some of the more curious regulatory changes that were considered and are currently in court are those pertaining to the assurance that companies which are mining on public lands or engaged in offshore drilling must prove they have enough money to clean up when the mines are played out and the oil wells run dry. In other words, when no longer profitable, a company can just walk away from its mess.

Other changes called for infrastructure designs to take into account weather changes and rising sea-levels. Regulations placing animals on endangered species lists are also being attacked. I hope the *New York Times* keeps this reference online for a long time.

---

79   https://www.nytimes.com/interactive/2019/climate/trump-environment-rollbacks.html

What the article doesn't discuss are the regulations that aren't being considered, like those restricting or even out phasing out such chemicals as glyphosate or neonicotinoid insecticides.

The reasons for some of these changes, such as limiting environmental impact studies to one year and 150 pages, are under the guise of reducing paperwork. The true conservative in me remains skeptical.

Some groups point out that India and China are given much greater leeway in the international accords than are the economies of North America and Europe. That may be so, but it should not give license to the rest of the world to ignore what is happening. The answer to that should be a preference given regarding import licenses and tariffs to manufacturers who prove they use a certain amount of renewable or other non-carbon-based energy. This rubs slightly against my beliefs in free trade; but countries that manufacture or ship with non-renewable, highly polluting fuels are hardly playing on a level field.

Reversing the policies of the EPA may result in short-term gain for some industries such as fossil fuels and transportation, but it will result in higher costs in the long run as the taxpayers have to live with increased levels of illness, more damage from storms, and a drop in biodiversity so we can have cheap gasoline.

The EPA's policies have affected nearly every single American and a lot of people outside the United States as well. Its rules have changed open sewers back into pleasant waterways, made city air more breathable, and returned dead lakes and ponds back to life. In my opinion, attacking the agency and its policies or staffing it with people who don't believe in its mission makes absolutely no sense. The agency should be allowed to pursue its intended goals and continue to improve our lives.

To get an idea of what America was like before the EPA the Popular Science site has an excellent pictorial. [80]

The Green New Deal

If you've been reading this book from the beginning, it's obvious that many of the opinions and research I've presented make me seem a bit divergent from what many consider to be the conservative orthodoxy. The Green New Deal is one more topic to add to that list.

It's not that I support the Green New Deal as it's written. I don't. However, there are some ideas in there that have merit and should be discussed. I also have suggestions on getting a lot of the GND fulfilled in a manner in which to get more people behind it, accomplish its goals, and do it without a major transformation of our economy.

As divisive as the GND resolution seems to be, very few people seem to have actually read it, so I will be critiquing a document for which some readers have no point of reference. I strongly recommend reading the full text as presented to Congress (see appendix B).[81]

A word about what the GND is *not*: It is not a bill that anyone plans to enact into law, it is a Congressional resolution.

80   https://www.popsci.com/america-before-epa-photos/?utm_source=internal&utm_medium=email

81   Available online at https://www.congress.gov/bill/116th-congress/house-resolution/109/text

A resolution in Congress is meant to voice the opinion of one or both chambers of Congress. The House of Representatives and the Senate can pass a resolution with or without the other chamber or a resolution could be joint, having been introduced by a member or members of the House or Senate to their respective chambers. The president does not act on resolutions and, again, they have no force of law. In general, parliamentary-style resolutions are not comprehensive diagrams of how the government should bring about change. It is merely a statement of ideals held by its sponsors and the members that voted in its favor.

The title "Green New Deal" is a bit of political marketing. It has the nostalgia of the era of Franklin Roosevelt pulling America out of the Great Depression and then bringing the nation to world prominence by leading us through most of World War II. The word "green," as everyone knows, is used to denote a positive influence on the environment.

Now for a bit of historical lore. FDR's New Deal was actually mentioned in a campaign speech as "a new deal" for the American public. America was currently mired in the most severe economic crisis since our founding and the speech was to promise a plan to get people back to work and the economy back on track. The term "New Deal" caught on quickly and became the theme for the presidency. Some liked its allusion to the "Square Deal" of President Theodore Roosevelt, the man who helped lead the nation into the modern economy and did so while controlling some major corporations that were quickly becoming monopolies whose existence could have hampered economic growth.

The New Deal was born of political necessity. With nearly half the nation out of work, industries were collapsing and farm prices were falling to a point that it wasn't worth the labor to grow crops or bring dairy products to market. The nation turned to FDR to come up with some answers.

The set of programs that became the structure of the New Deal were designed to provide some relief to people through work programs, welfare aid, and even public works projects to give people real work so they could earn their wages. Government agencies were formed to regulate what business remained and to control production in certain industries.

There have been hundreds, possibly thousands, of books written about FDR and his economic programs so I won't get into too much detail here. I will say that, while many of the era's agencies and organizations are long gone, there are still some in business—the Tennessee Valley Authority and Social Security, to name two.[82]

Like FDR's New Deal, the Green New Deal resolution is a reaction to what some perceive to be a crisis or series of crises.

The resolution begins simply enough. Like many resolutions, it is self-referential. It summarizes what the message of the resolution will be when it's passed. If it isn't passed, it's not really a resolution. It states at the top:

RESOLUTION

Recognizing the duty of the Federal Government to create a Green New Deal.

The resolution then opens by citing findings of the Intergovernmental Panel on Climate Change, a committee within the United Nations. The panel has reason to believe that the climate change that seemed to start, or accelerate, in the twentieth century is caused by human action.

---

82   In addition to some agencies still in business, there remain tangible reminders of some of the work of the New Deal. For more information, visit this website dedicated to preserving WPA and CCC projects: https://livingnewdeal.org

It's hard to argue with the presumed causes of climate change through the past 125 years. Although there is no definitive proof, the data suggest a strong correlation between the rise in global temperature and the industrialization of most of the world—in particular, the burning of fossil fuels to provide energy since the beginning of the Industrial Revolution.

Among the effects of climate change specified are rising sea levels and increases in wildfires, storms, droughts, and other severe weather events. The fact that those events are happening can be personally witnessed; one observes the increased frequency of severe storms in the United States and the annual increase in number of acres of land consumed by wildfires. (Australia set records for wildfires in their summer of 2019-2020.)

The eventual rise in temperature will result in major demographic and population shifts and people being displaced as their current homelands become undesirable or unable to sustain their needs. The GND proponents believe there will be other consequences, both for nature and for the economies of the world.

The proposed resolution then provides the submitters' justification as to why the U.S. should take the lead or at least make the GND part of national policy. They point out the U.S. has produced an outsized share of global pollution when compared to its population.

Some of the controversy the GND has generated lies in Section 4, by the wording in the following statement: "The United States must take a leading role in reducing emissions through economic transformation." I don't believe the majority of Americans have a problem with our nation taking the lead; it's the phrase "economic transformation" which raises suspicion.

That statement is followed by lists of what are claimed to be related crises. Among those cited are access to services and basic needs, for which (I believe) actual causation by climate change would be difficult to prove: declining life expectancy, access to clean water, food, health care, and so forth.

The statement that "climate change, pollution, and environmental destruction have exacerbated systemic racial, regional, social, environmental, end economic injustices" and affects certain demographic groups more than others certainly has merit and needs to be addressed both in the United States and the rest of the world. In my opinion, these are issues we all would like to see addressed, but the resolution's submitters are using the need for action on global warming as a reason to bundle issues that may be best addressed separately. This, combined with the phrase "economic transformation" seems to imply that this proposal calls for a major increase in the powers of the federal government.

That said, there is more of the Green New Deal resolution with which I agree.

Whereas, climate change constitutes a direct threat to the national security of the United States—

(1) by impacting the economic, environmental, and social stability of countries and communities around the world; and

(2) by acting as a threat multiplier...

The U.S. military has to be prepared for problems that will happen because of climate change.[83] The Department of Defense has been studying this issue for years. Less ice in the Arctic presents problems for the Navy, as it counters the

83   "Report on Effects of a Changing Climate to the Department of Defense," January 2019

forces of possible belligerent nations. The State Department and the Department of Defense will have to be on watch for unrest in nations that may be affected by water shortages as mountains receive less snow and glaciers that have fed rivers for centuries slowly disappear.[84] "Bad weather days" are increasing notably in certain parts of the world, which affects Air Force logistics and supply efforts in those regions.

The Army and ground forces of the Marine Corps have always prepared to fight in any terrain, but climate change that may transform swamps to forest and forest to desert over the years. Strategies will have to be regularly updated.

The GND resolution says that, with the current crises, we can take advantage of an opportunity of historic proportion and, almost nostalgically, compare it to our efforts to end the Great Depression and mobilization for World War II.

Let's jump back to the discussion of the FDR era. When the people of the United States mobilized military and civilian organizations to counter the threat of fascism, some groups were left out or relegated to less desirable positions. Military units were segregated, blacks in the Navy were often only cooks or orderlies, and the army had separate segregated units. Americans of Japanese descent faced a host of sanctioned discriminatory practices ranging from being refused defense jobs or losing existing jobs to being interned on the West Coast. Military women were relegated to clerical roles or nursing. These are valuable and essential jobs, of course, but some of these individuals might have been better used in other capacities.

Much has changed in eighty years. Such discrimination is now illegal. We have existing laws giving some preferences to

---

84   The Mekong River in Southeast Asia, the scene of a lot of fighting in the Vietnam War, has its headwaters in Himalayas.

women- and minority-owned businesses. I'm not so naïve to believe that racism and sexism have been eliminated in this country, but now there is legal recourse. Adding more laws and bureaucracy won't make the remaining problems go away; it will just add red tape as organizations and companies are forced to prove they don't discriminate in hiring, promotions, and pay. The best thing to do is to enforce the existing laws. That will help insure equal access to the opportunities afforded.

The GND's proponents call for a ten-year national mobilization to achieve the goals of self-sufficiency through the establishment of 100 percent clean and renewable energy sources and address other issues contained in the document.

Once the United States achieves the goals (or at least is well on the way to achievement), the resolution calls for the sharing of technology with other nations. This may be a problem, for some technology is the intellectual property of individuals or corporations. If such an agreement is made to share technology, those who spent the time and effort in development are going to want fair compensation.

As critical as I may be, many of the goals described in the GND are for the most part achievable but not solely by an overreaching federal government. Many can be achieved independently and by private industry. Earlier in this book I talked about the tax laws, low-cost leases of federal land, and minimal royalties earned by states that support the fossil fuel industry. Phasing out such benefits so that all competitors in the energy industry (and supporting industries) play by the same rules as renewable energy companies will make the latter a much better financial investment. One example: by definition, renewable energy companies can't claim a depletion of resources.

Guaranteeing jobs with certain set wages and defined benefits is never a good idea. It discourages the individual initiative that benefits both employee and employer. Any jobs should be at market wages and competitive benefits. This is not a criticism of minimum wage laws but a criticism of pay and benefit guarantees without regard to merit.

(I) strengthening and protecting the right of all workers to organize, unionize, and collectively bargain free of coercion, intimidation, and harassment;

Section (I) is, in my opinion, included in the GND as quoted above in order to get the support of labor union leadership. Workers should have the right to organization and in collective bargaining. Conversely, in my opinion, it should also be a right of workers to not belong to a union or other collective bargaining unit. The people not wanting to be in a union should also be guaranteed protection from the harassment of unions, as union organizers would be protected from harassment by management.

(N) ensuring a commercial environment where every businessperson is free from unfair competition and domination by domestic or international monopolies; and

(O) providing all people of the United States with—

(i) high-quality health care;

(ii) affordable, safe, and adequate housing;

(iii) economic security; and

(iv) clean water, clean air, healthy and affordable food, and access to nature.

The above items (N) and (O) are also good ideas, but the means will be debated for some time to come. Of course, two terms used here are particularly ambiguous: "affordable" and "nature."

Not every government program is a failure or underperforms, and New Deal programs were no exception. Two programs that were part of the New Deal's effort to ensure equal access to resources and control dangerous conditions created by nature were the Tennessee Valley Authority (TVA) and the Rural Electrification Act (REA). The TVA was intended to control some of the flooding in the Tennessee Valley area through construction projects which addressed a secondary goal—to provide electricity to areas that had none. The REA helped fund the formation and the mission of rural co-ops to bring electricity to small towns and farms around the country.

These agencies still exist today. Why? Because they had clearly defined goals and they still carry out their mission. If politicians were to enact legislation to carry out some of the goals of the GND, they would do well to follow the model of agencies with clear missions and discrete areas of responsibility. (More on this issue later.)

The Senate has already voted down the Green New Deal resolution, and I doubt it will ever pass. This doesn't mean that I don't think some of the goals are admirable. Congress needs to promote renewable or carbon-free energy sources, and it can do so by leveling the playing field between those sources and the fossil fuel industry.

While the Green New Deal's authors try to compare it to some of the great efforts of the 1930s and 1940s, they do not seem to recognize that those efforts were to deal with immediate threats whose effects were being felt then and there—in particular, economic depression and the rise of international fascism. The goal of the New Deal was clear: to get people to work. The resulting Civilian Conservation

Corps and the Work Projects Administration produced the short-term results of providing a paycheck and restoring dignity to many workers. It also left long-lasting results in the form of improved infrastructure and civic buildings that stand to this day. There are even works of art produced through these programs that continue to inspire us.

But the nation's leaders knew that they had an end in mind. Once Hitler and the Japanese empire were defeated, the military would be downsized. Once people were back to work, many of the New Deal programs would end. Government planning and centralized authority of industries would be eliminated.

Fighting the rise of fascism resulted in the United States becoming one of two superpowers on the planet. These effects are, too, still felt today.

What the Green New Deal writers should propose is something more along the lines of Eisenhower's push for a national highway system or Kennedy's push for a massive space program. We knew that we would eventually finish the highways and reach the moon, but transportation and space exploration are still part of our culture. Reaching the goals of an interstate highway system and the space program may have been inspired by an individual's vision, but the achievement wasn't the result of one man taking central leadership but the government, businesses large and small, and private individuals working toward common goals.

Rather than calling for a ten-year mobilization we should be looking for permanent partnerships between government and industry to push for a permanent change in our culture where the goals are energy independence, a cleaner environment, and protections put into place to make sure that everyone has clean air, water, and access to education—because it will require skilled people to create and maintain such an environment. And everyone should have a chance to prosper.

There are no guarantees in life, and I don't think guaranteed jobs or income are the way to go. The best course of action is to make sure everyone understands the goal and has an opportunity to work and get a chance to share in that prosperity.

Unfortunately, the Green New Deal was introduced by one party without prior input from the opposition. Nothing of substance will get accomplished until the leaders of the major parties sit down and discuss what they have in common before working on the areas of disagreement. Then, something might be accomplished that would benefit all.

Food waste

Stop criticizing those not eating meat: they may be right[85]

There's a lot of intolerance in this world (another obvious statement in a book that seems full of them). So much of it is based on political, racial, or religious differences. It's been around for millennia, and isn't about to stop soon.

There is one type of intolerance that I just can't fathom, however, and it hasn't been around that long: the intolerance

85   https://www.popsci.com/vegan-high-protein-foods/?utm_source=internal&utm_medium=email

for people who eat differently than oneself. I don't mean people who keep kosher or follow other religious dietary directives, although I have heard snide remarks made about them. I am referring to the widespread intolerance toward those following vegetarian or vegan diets.

I don't like to call people vegan or vegetarian. Identifying people by their diet doesn't make a lot of sense. Would you introduce someone at a party as "Phil, a Weight Watcher"?

Some people follow certain diets as part of a religious faith. The majority following vegetarian and vegan diets in the United States do it for other reasons as well, however. Some believe it is cruel to raise animals just to eat them or, in the case of someone following a vegan diet, it is cruel to consume any animal product or use it for clothing or other purposes. I think everyone should respect others' reasons.

I'm not one to really care what someone else eats. I do wonder how one gets all the needed nutrients on a vegan diet, but most of the people I know following such regimens are intelligent and capable of doing their own research and creating their own menus.[86]

So why do so many people (verbally) attack people on a vegan or vegetarian regimen? Or think it's funny or some solemn duty of theirs to try and trick these people into consuming some sort of meat, dairy, or egg product? Honestly, I have no idea. That is one for the psychologists to figure out.

Maybe it's time to look at some of the differences in diets—not in terms of nutrients received, but in effects on the environment. Because, when you come right down to it, vegetarian or vegan diets may be the way to go.

---

86   https://www.popsci.com/vegan-high-protein-foods/?utm_
source=internal&utm_medium=email

First let's discuss water, the most essential ingredient in food production. In New England, droughts are measured in weeks or months. Water is plentiful and lakes, ponds, streams, and rivers abound. In most of eastern Massachusetts you don't have to dig too far down to find enough water for a well. If towns have water problems, they are usually infrastructure-based, not for lack of supply. In other parts of the continent it's a different story: Droughts are measured in years and, even with regular rainfall, surface water is not always naturally plentiful.

Using technology—some modern, some dating back to the ancient Romans—farmers have been able to overcome problems with obtaining water. I know it's not always easy and there are times even the best technology won't save crops, but for the most part, farmers and their crops and livestock survive.

All this being true, the diets of most modern North Americans, from Mexico to Canada, are extremely water intensive. Let's look at milk and the beverages that are offered as its substitutes such as almond and soy milks.[87]

How much fresh water it takes to produce a certain product seems to depend on your data sources. It also depends on when you start the meter. Some information starts tallying the water for cows' milk from the day a calf is born and accounts for the water for its feed and the water required to process it all along the way. For the almond industry, some estimates start with the growing of an almond tree.

Each industry has its own reason for presenting data in a certain way, and there has been some misinformation

---

87   There is some contention to referring to plant-based beverages and foods with the same name as their counterparts. For example, some may refute that plant-based yogurt can be called yogurt, as it normally contains dairy.

from both the sides of dairy farmers and of milk substitute manufacturers. Thus, any information I present should be kept in perspective.

Almonds, especially those used to make—for lack of a better term—almond milk, are often vilified. Water quantities of up to 1.1 gallons are often quoted to produce one almond.[88] Other sources talk about 300 gallons of water to produce a gallon of almond milk. The same sources claim it takes 977 gallons of water to produce one gallon of cows' milk.

No matter your source, almond milk requires less water than cows' milk.[89] The other comparisons you can make when comparing a vegan diet to a more omnivorous diet revolve around the other resources involved. When looking into the affects on the environment for food production fuel, fertilizer, and byproducts (like bovine-produced methane) must be considered.

Trading cows' milk for an almond- or soy-based substitute may seem to be a big step but it's only one type of substitution. For years, vegetarian and vegan cookbooks have offered alternatives to meat, particularly beef, but really couldn't offer anything with the flavor or texture of beef. In the past few years, however, several companies have brought forward what seems to be a flavorful beef substitute. Even major restaurant chains have embraced the products, placing them prominently on their menus.

What is the difference between beef and beef substitutes when it comes to water consumption? Like with the debate of the almond milk versus cows' milk, estimates vary. The

---

88   https://www.theguardian.com/lifeandstyle/shortcuts/2015/oct/21/almond-milk-quite-good-for-you-very-bad-for-the-planet

89   The nutritional comparison is quite different. Everyone needs to do their own research to meet their needs.

website EatThis.com discussed what the meat substitute called "Impossible" is and isn't. The claim is that Impossible uses only 450 gallons of water per pound of the product, which compares favorably to the 1,800 gallons for a pound of beef.[90] Similar information is discussed in other articles.[91]

Water is just one resource to be considered when comparing a food supply's effects on the planet. Other issues to consider are land use, wastes produced, and energy both producing and transporting per pound of food. A vegetable-based diet compares favorably on all counts.

I'm not saying the world needs to convert to a diet of vegetables. I would certainly miss burgers, steaks, and other meats. But contemplating such a diet does make one aware of what it takes to put that meatloaf on the table. So maybe stop being so critical when your new neighbors politely decline your signature barbecue ribs and sauce at the neighborhood cookout. Maybe you could be more understanding and not take their refusal as an insult.

Light pollution: from an astronomer's nuisance to an ecological threat

Human beings love light. Before Edison, Tesla, and Westinghouse made the generation and transmission of electricity for artificial lighting practical, humans were at

90   https://www.eatthis.com/facts-about-the-impossible-burger

91   https://www.fastcompany.com/90322572/heres-how-the-footprint-of-the-plant-based-impossible-burger-compares-to-beef

constant war with darkness—and with the inventions of the late nineteenth and early twentieth century, humans seem to be winning. But this victory may be at a cost.

Before electric light there were campfires, candles, lanterns, and gas lighting. None were nearly as efficient or safe as electrical lighting. Except for being tired when it was time to go to work, electric lighting was seen as a boon to civilization. We are safer and more in control of our schedules, no longer dependent on the sun alone for the illumination to make extended workdays possible, thus increasing our productivity.

A few decades ago, we started hearing about light pollution. Not many people seemed to consider our artificial lights as a threat to our lives. The amplified difficulty of seeing the stars in the night sky seemed like a problem limited to astronomers. The increase in artificial lighting came so gradually over the last century that urban and suburban dwellers didn't even notice the lack of stars until they took a vacation far away from their city or town. Then they looked up at the night sky in amazement. When vacation ended and it was time to head back to the seas of artificial outdoor lighting, they shrugged their shoulders and said they would miss the stars like they would miss a mountain vista or a roaring ocean. It's something that's nice to see because you don't have it at home, but you don't see the possibility of everyone turning off the outdoor lights at night.

That started changing in the eighties. I don't know what the catalyst was that got everyone organized; maybe it was satellite photographs of industrialized countries at night that showed cities, towns, and highways glowing like they were their own astronomical objects. Not only did we realize why we couldn't see any but the brightest stars, planets, and the moon; we also acknowledged that we were obviously wasting energy and money lighting up the bottoms of satellites.

In the late eighties, International Dark-Sky Organization was formed with the goal of reducing light pollution.[92] They have been making progress since then. Government organizations that oversee street lighting and regulate the building codes are also getting behind the idea of requiring or at least encouraging the use of dark-sky compliant lighting fixtures.

While many thought the Dark-Sky Organization was a good idea on the merit of re-opening the night sky to humans, there may be another benefit. Over the past twenty years there has been a noticeable drop in overall insect biomass in many regions. Anecdotally speaking, you may have noticed it because you haven't had to clean your windshield and front bumper as often as your parents did or you don't see fireflies lighting up your backyard on a summer evening as often as you used to.

The drop in insect biomass used to get blamed on the indiscriminate use of pesticides and the destruction of insect-friendly habitats. These are still major factors, but recent research suggests that a third factor involved in the loss of fireflies is light pollution.[93] Artificial outdoor light confuses many insects and interferes with their normal feeding and mating routines. Artificial light may also make it easier for some insectivores to find their prey at night. Other insectivores that don't take advantage of artificial light may be experiencing a drop in population—and the effects go on.

Fewer insects can have an effect on local plant life. Some nocturnal insects are pollinators for many wild plants and

---

92   https://www.darksky.org
93   https://www.theguardian.com/environment/2020/feb/22/why-lights-going-out-fireflies-conservation-pollution

trees. Fewer insects means less efficient reproduction for important plants and trees.

By following the guidelines of the IDA, we may be able to return access to the night sky for millions of people around the world and help restore the insect biomass (along with reductions in pesticide use and easing the destruction of insect habitats).

Over time, maybe suburban backyard astronomy won't be limited to just the moon and the brightest planets, and neighborhood kids chasing fireflies at dusk will be a reality more than a memory. Of course, you may have to spend more time cleaning your car's windshield.

QUICK HITS AND SHORT RANTS

Following are some quick opinions that will pop up randomly and apropos of nothing in particular.

Cynical charitable advertising

Have you ever been watching television and seen a commercial come on announcing that if you patronize a particular company, they will donate a certain amount of money to a charity, maybe even the charity of your choice? These come-ons can range from hundreds of dollars if you test-drive a car to a portion of the profits of a sale going to a certain cause.

I find such advertising a bit cynical. These companies' largess depends on you spending money. If a company really wants to impress me, I'd like to see them just give money to a charity instead. Then they can announce it in their ads; they can even fly a banner from their flagpole announcing their generosity. I would hold a company that did this in greater respect than those that demand you first spend money with them before they will donate.

Trophy hunting: I don't get it

I have a friend who is very involved with saving megafauna, especially apex predators, all over the world. She has brought to my attention the waste involved in trophy hunting.

I have nothing against hunting, per se. I understand that there are parts of the U.S., some not too far from wealthy cities, where some people's food budget includes a box of shells for their hunting rifle. Getting some ducks or a deer will mean a good source of protein for the family. What I don't get is people who will travel great distances to shoot a large and, in some cases, threatened animal.

What great skill and bravery does it show to fly thousands of miles, climb into a truck or helicopter, and be driven to a place where your prey has already been spotted for you, handed a preloaded rifle, and given the sole job of aiming and pulling the trigger? Just to see an elephant or giraffe fall.

Some readers may consider me a bit of a hypocrite since I praise Teddy Roosevelt for being a conservative conservationist though he is also known as a big game hunter. There are a couple of key differences. Hunters in Roosevelt's day had to endure hardship and travel to get to the hunting grounds. Some even considered it a form of research to bring back preserved specimens of a great beast. Fortunately, we have better ways to study megafauna than destroying it.

Plastic fashion

How green are your clothes? Okay, that's a lame attempt at an environmental pun. We're donning more plastic than ever, it seems. Nylon, polyester, Lycra, and even polyvinyl chloride being marketed as vegetarian leather. Modern synthetics differ from what was available in the seventies and eighties. They are more comfortable and, to some, look better. Microfiber is used for towels and perspiration-absorbing athletic clothing. But no matter what you call it, it's actually plastic.

Earlier in this book I mentioned issues with microplastics. One of the sources of these problematic microplastics is our clothing. When synthetic plastics wear out, it is usually because the material is abrading. Just like natural fibers, we don't notice the tiny particles of plastic sloughing off as our favorite shirt or pair of pants turns threadbare. Unlike the particles of silk, linen, or cotton which don't build up in the environment as they are eventually decomposed by natural means, plastic particles don't break down as readily and instead will remain in the environment for centuries to come.

Washing synthetic fabrics also adds to this microplastic build-up. Perhaps someone will invent an improved lint filter in both washers and dryers to mitigate this issue somewhat. Need I say this—if you wear a lot of synthetics, don't put dryer lint out for birds to use as nesting material. And if your personal budget allows, stick with natural fabrics in your wardrobe.

Organic food... in plastic wrap

A friend of mine brought this issue up recently over lunch. She wondered aloud about the packaging that protects our food. So many stores today offer organic vegetables, fruits, and even eggs with a minimum of packaging. Yet the larger chains that have started carrying these same organic foods haven't quite caught on to the packaging problem yet. My local supermarket sells organic produce... wrapped in difficult-to-recycle plastic film. The organically fed, cage-free eggs come in plastic or plastic foam cartons even though biodegradable cardboard cartons have been around since... well, since chicken eggs went to market.

I'm sure the markets will figure it out eventually.

GLOBAL WARMING

Global warming, or climate change, has been on people's minds for what seems like a couple of decades now. The two terms are used interchangeably to indicate the same concept: The average temperature of the Earth is rising, and the rate of this rise is accelerating. Although the amounts talked about seem small, the effects will be felt by everyone. Researchers talk about an increase by one or two degrees Celsius in the average annual temperature. Because of this temperature rise, Arctic ice is not forming in the same quantities of past generations, glaciers seem to be melting, and invasive species of plants and animals are moving into areas that were, until recently, inhospitable to them.

There are three questions that are asked constantly in regard to this global warming problem, and rightfully so, as everyone should be thinking about them:

- Is global warming real?
- What is causing it?
- Is it really a threat?

Is global warming real?

There seems to be a consensus among both skeptics and believers: The data from the past hundred years or so seem to support the hypothesis that global warming is real. The disagreements come in the rate of acceleration, the time period over which the warming trend will continue, and whether or not it is a normal part of the Earth's cycles.

Consider this saying attributed to author Robert A. Heinlein: "Climate is what you expect. Weather is what you get." Residents of New England expect strong variations in the climate. But in the past few decades, the winters have seen greatly varying amounts of snow and what seem to be wilder fluctuations in temperature. Summer storms are getting stronger and more frequent.

But if you refuse to believe the data, how about your own memory?

I remember a winter in New England that seemed to prove that the Earth was cooling. In February of that year it seemed we were out of school for three weeks due to inclement weather. In reality it was nearly two weeks because our scheduled February vacation was in there—but nonetheless, the snow was quite real.

I keep referring to the place I grew up as relatively rural. We used to sled on nearby hills and ice skate, safely, on local ponds and lakes sometimes as soon as Thanksgiving but definitely before Christmas. There were also functioning ski slopes and lifts in southeastern Massachusetts and Rhode Island that would operate whenever there was natural snow available. Several towns in my area had slopes served by a ski lift. The season wasn't as long as it is in New Hampshire and vertical drops were measured in hundreds, not thousands, of feet, but it was still skiing.[94]

I concede that it wasn't climate alone that killed these local slopes; improved transportation and economic factors led to the demise of some of them. But over time, the lack of snow made running lifts and maintaining slopes by volunteers impractical. The nearest one to me was last operated about twenty-five years ago.

Sledding season is much shorter now, and the evening news regularly warns of the dangers of pond skating. (Although, to be fair, the local evening news thrives on giving their audience something to worry about.) All things considered, this is my anecdotal evidence that things have changed and most likely are still changing.

In defense of skeptics, some may say you can't blame people for their confusion on the issue of global temperature changes. After all, when I was in school back in the 1960s there were stories in the popular media that the Earth was on a cooling trend. I was too young to be reading scientific papers, but even the popular magazines of the time talked about the possibility of a coming ice age and what could be done to prevent glaciers from forming and destroying our way of life. Among the proposed action was to somehow darkening large areas of the planet to help trap heat.[95] *Harper's Magazine* published a well researched article on the subject.[96]

It turns out the data on cooling was misleading and had led to erroneous conclusions. The trend is warming instead. One group recently finished a study on the length of winter in the northern United States and southern Canada,

---

94   http://www.nelsap.org/ma/sunrise.html
95   https://harpers.org/archive/1958/09/the-coming-ice-age/
96   https://harpers.org/archive/1958/09/the-coming-ice-age/

primarily the states and provinces surrounding the Great Lakes, New England, and New Brunswick. The Ecological Society of Americas studied various factors and conditions that constitute what many consider winter.[97] (I urge you to read the full report. Unlike a lot of scientific papers, this one is extremely accessible to the lay person.)

In this study, factors included days defined by temperature, snowpack, and the effect of the ground not freezing. The study is interesting in that it not only discusses the harmful effects of a shorter, milder winter—such as invasive plants native to warmer areas moving northward—but also some beneficial effects such as more growth time for native trees and brush.

The study includes other effects that we don't always think of: the direct economic effects. When the ground is frozen, foresters and loggers can get into more remote areas for harvesting timber. Frozen ground is relatively stable ground, and damage to heavy trucks and timber harvesting equipment is minimized. Fewer days with a solid frozen ground can lead to soil instability. Logging equipment can get bogged down and become unable to function efficiently. The instability of the soil can lead to tree root damage, limiting the growth of trees for future harvests.

Why should we believe today's research over the climate cooling research of the mid-twentieth century? One reason is that today's climatologists enjoy a few advantages that researchers fifty years ago did not. Data is gathered in more locations and in more detail than ever before. Modern researchers have access to computing power that

97   Alexandra R. Contosta, Nora J. Casson, Sarah Garlick, Sarah J. Nelson, Matthew P. Ayres, Elizabeth A. Burakowski, John Campbell, Irena Creed, et al, "Northern forest winters have lost cold, snowy conditions that are important for ecosystems and human communities," first published July 16, 2019, https://doi.org/10.1002/eap.1974

their predecessors could only dream of. Using this data and the computing power models, everything seems to point to temperatures increasing. The only disagreement seems to be the rate of increase and the extent. It also points out that certain insects' lives are extended by stretches of warm weather, which means more damage to trees from boring insects and other pests.

Maybe you don't believe the data or feel that it might be subject to interpretation to achieve a political aim. I could start quoting studies about climate change, the infamous "hockey stick" graph showing temperature changes since the turn of the last century—but would you believe them?

Maintaining a healthy skepticism is a very positive thing. Maybe there are reasons for scientists and researchers to interpret the data in ways that prove their own points. Aren't we all human? Don't we all have certain prejudices, conscious and subconscious? Of course we do. There is always the possibility that someone who stands to gain will finance studies until one comes up with the data that helps the world to see things their intended way. But in the case of climate change, multiple studies show the same or at least similar results.

For fans of old television—remember the glacier story from the Alfred Hitchcock television series?[98] It was a classic episode in which a young bride becomes a widow six months into her marriage when her husband dies while glacier-climbing in the Austrian Alps. She is shocked to be informed that his body was lost in a glacial crevasse and cannot be recovered. The young woman consults a glaciologist who tells her that his body will eventually emerge from the glacier

---

98   https://www.imdb.com/title/tt0508277/

some forty years down the road. She vows to not marry again until his body is recovered.

The episode wasn't meant to be a lesson in geography and glaciology, but rather just a typical Hitchcock suspense story. It does, however, show us that at one time the melt rate of glaciers was predictable—probably not to the accuracy level of the month and year an object would reappear from a glacier's innards—but predictable to a fair extent. Glaciers were also sustained by regular snowfalls.

Today, glaciers are melting faster than they can be replenished. That body would be showing up a lot sooner.

What is causing it?

If you accept that global warming is real—and I have a feeling that if you didn't, you would have stopped reading this chapter already—the next question is, "What is its cause?" That's the question that is at the root of most of the debate. There are a number of reasons cited by various groups, some more reasonable than others. Among them are:

- Increased levels of methane and carbon dioxide, gasses that are often referred to as "greenhouse gasses" because of their ability to help trap heat in the Earth's atmosphere.
- Changes in activity of the sun. It was erroneously reported a few years back that other planets were also being warmed along with the Earth.
- Variations in the Earth's rotation or its orbit.

Skeptics maintain that the weather changes and average temperature increases are just natural changes in the planet's cycles and humans have nothing to do with it.

In the past two millennia, the Earth has experienced periods of warming and cooling that have had effects on human events. Theories about the causes abound, among them changes in solar activity, increased volcanic activity, and changes in ocean currents. One factor that was not a primary cause in the far past was the release of greenhouse gasses by the burning of fossil fuels. That is unique to the past two hundred years or so when humans first began burning coal, oil, and natural gas.

Perhaps our current period of warming is caused by a combination of factors and not solely by anthropologic activity. No matter the cause or causes, we have to be prepared for the consequences.

A side note: Even if you don't believe global warming is caused by human activity, it still couldn't hurt to start investing in renewable energy that can be produced domestically. In an earlier chapter I talked about all of the bloodshed and economic blackmail that can be attributed to oil production. Removing oil, or at least lessening its influence on world politics, could only be good for the planet.

Is it a threat?

Are you convinced that the Earth is warming but wondering why you should care? Maybe milder winters appeal to you. Your heating bills will be lower, so you'll be saving energy, right? Well, despite warmer winters, be aware that the weather swings between hot and cold may intensify from season to season. But there's more to it. Here are some of the possible effects of a changing climate, in particular an increase in the average temperature:

- Sea level rising
- Heavier storms
- Damage to vulnerable cities
- Drought
- Desertification
- Political conflict over the control of water sources

These aren't the concerns of a few academics sitting in laboratories far removed from the average American; it's a major concern of the United States Department of Defense. (Also, it's mentioned in the text of the Green New Deal resolution.) The United States military recognizes this, and in 2019 they released a report citing a number of key military installations and cross-referenced it with several anticipated effects of climate change. The chart below is taken from that report.[99]

Summary Table of Current & Potential Effects to 79 Installations

The following tables provide a summary of current and future (20 years) vulnerabilities to military installations.[3]

Service	# Installations	Recurrent Flooding		Drought		Desertification		Wildfires		Thawing Permafrost	
		Current	Potential	Current	Potential	Current	Potential	Current	Potential	Current	Potential
Air Force	36	20	25	20	22	4	4	32	32	-	-
Army	21	15	17	5	5	2	2	4	4	1	1
Navy	18	16	16	18	18	-	-	-	7	-	-
DLA	2	2	2	-	2	-	-	-	-	-	-
DFAS	1	-	-	-	1	-	-	-	-	-	-
WHS	1	-	-	-	-	-	-	-	-	-	-
Totals	79	53	60	43	48	6	6	36	43	1	1

---

99   "Report on Effects of a Changing Climate to the Department of Defense," January 2019

A review of this chart indicates that recurrent flooding, drought, desertification, and wildfires are the primary concerns at the 79 installations included in the analysis.

It isn't just the installations that are at risk. Actual warfighting strategy will be affected. Equipment designed for desert fighting will be needed in areas where it hasn't been used before. Soil will become unstable, meaning some vital equipment will be bogged down and made immobile.

The CIA, Pentagon, and several other institutions within the federal government feel global warming is real and has potentially profound effects.

Let's look at the civilian side of things. For the past hundred years we've built up an infrastructure for what we expect to happen. There have been headlines making exceptions, but for the most part the arrangements in place have suited us well. If global warming happens at an accelerated rate, as some predict, our infrastructure will be subject to damage before we can replace it through normal maintenance. Much of this damage could happen because of the increased occurrences of hundred-year storms.[100]

If you are concerned about what is happening to Earth's climate, there are all sorts of action you can take. But, while individual action to hinder the effects of global warming are important, it will take a unified effort to make a real difference. And this effort has to be made from the bottom up.

---

100 "Hundred-year storms" do not necessarily happen only once in a hundred years. Visit this webpage for a good explanation of the term: https://www.livescience.com/5751-100-year-storm.html

On doing your own research and believing what you want to believe

"Spin" is a popular term in the world of news and politics. I tried to find out when it entered our national vocabulary. While I couldn't find a precise date, I figured out it seemed to come into popularity in the 1990s. It was so much on our minds that it was used in the name of a politically-oriented situation comedy.

Spin is the art of taking a story from the media or from your own sources, admitting to the facts, and then turning the facts to support your narrative of an event. Usually it means trying to turn the story into a positive. This happens every day when someone from the news media sticks a microphone in front of a politician, but some have turned it into a real art form. The name of the musical group the Spin Doctors is derived from a term for a public relations specialist, usually a member of a politician's staff, who is charged with putting a negative story in the best possible light.

People tend to believe what they want to believe—and people are turning to internet sources for what they hope are the facts. The internet gives us the ability to access troves of information.[101] It also gives us the ability to pick and choose the information we need to support our own beliefs and support our own arguments.

You can find "proof" to deny major man-made horrors like the Holocaust ever happened or that the government communicates regularly with extra-terrestrials or reasons that your favorite politician should be nominated for sainthood. We can usually find what we want arranged in fifteen second

---

101   In this context I am using the term information to mean downloadable text, pictures, and video – not whether or not the data are actually true.

soundbites, five-minute videos and neatly bulleted "Five Things You Need To…" articles.

If you are involved in any of the popular social media platforms you have seen articles and videos on all sorts of these subjects—and saving the planet is just one of them.

Websites that perpetuate misleading articles and place incredible spin on various topics are well known on the Internet. They may have impressive, almost academic, sounding names and even have videos hosted by people with some impressive credentials. Information presented may be partly true or part of the truth. It all depends on how much spin is used.

I watched one video and really wasn't sure if they were trying to make a serious point or if it was some work of satire video, much like the *The Onion*, a media source that some people don't know is satirical.

One popular video refers to fossil fuels as the greenest of fuels because it adds to the atmosphere gasses upon with plants depend and tells us that satellite imagery shows the world is getting greener. It does not mention the fact that carbon dioxide is the gas.

Here's where spin comes in; the world is actually getting greener because snowpack is lessening, glaciers are melting, and species of plants are growing where they haven't in recorded history. Grass is being seen on Mount Everest and dandelions are growing on Mount Washington in New Hampshire.

Another video may claim that the increase in fossil fuels over the last thirty years correlates with greater portions of the population having access to clean water. Remember what your high school statistics teacher told you – 'correlation is not causation'. The sanitation of water requires energy and until recently the only practical solution was fossil fuel which in many cases can now be replaced by other sources. Also, it has only been in the past couple of decades that investment has been made in water systems in poorer nations. As solar efficiency improves, we will see it replacing a lot of fossil fuel power plants.

With a little searching you can find videos explaining that fossil fuel is a form of solar energy because coal, oil, and natural gas required the suns energy to form. That is rue if one goes back the millions of years to the carbon-based microorganisms that took in carbon dioxide and then expelled oxygen, thereby acting as a carbon sequestering system. What the proponents of fossil as solar fail to mention is that oil, coal, and natural gas are being burned faster than they could be ever be renewed by nature. Solar, maybe by the most stretched definition – sustainable, definitely not.

I suppose it's fun to play with semantics and split linguistic hairs.

I purposely don't mention the sites because I really have nothing to gain by being sued. So just as I encourage readers to be skeptical, I also encourage them to personally to some research and see what ridiculous misinformation is being disseminated throughout society.

If you run across information on an Internet source, do a little research before sharing it. If you can find a couple of independent sources to prove the veracity of what you want to share, then it probably is something that deserves to be shared.

If you can't find other sources then chances are it's someone's attempt at propaganda or, at worse, a malicious lie.

These are my rules:

GET INFO FROM MULTIPLE SOURCES.

WATCH OUT FOR THE SPIN

A PERSON IS NOT WRONG BECAUSE THEY DISAGREE WITH YOUR POLITICS

A PERSON IS NOT RIGHT BECAUSE THEY AGREE WITH YOUR POLITICS

‑‑‑||‑‑‑

Conclusion

Saving the planet is not something that's going to be done by the hero of a physics defying movie like "Voyage to the Bottom of the Sea" or "Armageddon." Both were fun movies and I will watch them when they are on TV, but it's not how things will work out.

Saving the planet from ourselves is going to be a combination of individual efforts, small group actions, businesses realizing there is profited to be made in sustainable practices, and some limited government regulation and law enforcement.

As a nation we will always have disagreements – it's part of our history. When I think about it if everyone thinks the same then you have one boring society.

When debating issues there are a couple traps to avoid.

Authority Bias - I'm probably guilty of this myself. We tend to take the word of someone who is seen as an authority as the end of discussion. We may even do that when the authority figure speaks out on issues in which they are not necessarily an authority. How many times have you realized a product exists, but you never really cared about it? Then one day your favorite actress or sports star appears on screen and all of a sudden you pay attention.

Several years ago, Fiat Chrysler reintroduced a classic model name that was applied to a brand-new automobile, the Dodge Dart. I might not have given it a second thought except the commercial showed briefly showed New England Patriots legend Tom Brady. I don't know if Brady ever sat down behind the wheel of a Dodge Dart – but all of a sudden it had my attention. Had I been in the market for a new compact car I might have considered the Dart.

Reverse Authority Bias or "Whatever it is, I'm against it."

Many years ago, I was employed at Harvard Medical School when the University was inaugurating a new president – I won't say which one because I don't want to embarrass him (he's still alive at the time of this writing). He was making the traditional calls upon all the schools within the university and eventually came to the HMS campus for an informal breakfast reception. I didn't expect to get more than a brief handshake and maybe thirty seconds about my role at the school.

I was pleasantly surprised when I bumped into him at the bagel table and we started discussing the challenges he faced heading up what many consider one of the world's most prestigious schools with a history going back to the colonial era.

If you've ever worked in academia you know that consensus is seldom seen. I asked him if he had ever seen the Marx Brothers' film "Horse Feathers." He had and he said he really enjoyed it. We discussed the movie and the scene where Groucho sings 'Whatever it is, I'm against it".

In that scene Groucho, as the newly appointed head of a university tells the faculty that whatever they propose – he will oppose. And that is reverse authority bias - You ignore the facts because of who is presenting them, no matter how well researched. You don't agree because you don't like the presenter. I am not a big fan of Donald Trump; I wasn't a fan of Barack Obama as president either. There are times I listen to speeches and think they are, as we used to say, "full of it". Other times I sit there and nod my head in agreement.

I'm sure after reading this book there are many who will say that I am not a true conservative since I do not agree completely with whomever it is these days who the arbiter of all things conservative. That is not true, I believe it is the duty of every conservative to think for him or herself and come to a decision based on the calculus of pros and cons. Actually – that is the duty of any intelligent person.

I still believe that the Constitution is the law of the land, that every person should be judged on his or her merits and not be pigeonholed by sex, race, or creed. I agree with the saying that the government that governs best, governs least (some attribute this to Jefferson some attribute it Henry David Thoreau). I want minimal taxes, but I admit the necessity of paying them.

At the same time, I understand that everything has a cost. (A clean environment, the military, education to name a few)

As a conservative - if you want to really be effective in saving the planet, team up with an educated liberal. I'm not necessarily talking about someone with an advanced degree from an elite university – although that might be helpful. I'm talking about someone who is well informed and researches issue and who agrees with you on the goals of sustainable business practices and responsible use of the planet's resources but, and this is important, disagrees on how to achieve those goals. If you're a liberal, find a conservative.

Then you can debate over lunch, a cup of coffee, or even a couple of beers. You will both learn something and then we have a fighting chance at keeping the planet safe from ourselves.

Just remember, when engaged in a heated debate or argument it is okay to attack your opponent's ideas and even data sources. What causes a breakdown in communication is when you attack the person.

Follow these ideas and in the end – you will know more than you did before and maybe the last argument is who grabs the check.

One more quick rant: The weakest argument against conservation

There are some reasons why some people don't care about conservation and I have heard some arguments against it. Some people believe the planet can absorb whatever we throw at it, any changes are part of the cycles. Others say that environmental degradation is inevitable, why fight it.

One strange argument I've heard against conservation and for exploiting natural resources to their fullest extent regardless of the consequences is from someone who quote the Bible. (You may refer to the quote from Genesis at the beginning of this book)

In my unlearned opinion, what the Bible is saying is that by being granted dominion humans must take responsibility for what happens on the planet and protect its resources. There is no problem using the resources in a sustainable manner, but that means making sure that the world's resources are available for all in the current generation and will be there for future generations. It does not mean ruining the world for short term gain.

APPENDICES:

Appendix A

Abstract of "Northern forest winters have lost cold, snowy conditions that are important for ecosystems and human communities". (Northern forest winters have lost cold, snowy conditions that are important for ecosystems and human communities; Alexandra R. Contosta Nora J. Casson Sarah Garlick Sarah J. Nelson Matthew P. Ayres Elizabeth A. Burakowski John Campbell Irena Creed, et al, First published: 16 July 2019 https://doi.org/10.1002/eap.1974)

Winter is an understudied but key period for the socioecological systems of northeastern North American forests. A growing awareness of the importance of the winter season to forest ecosystems and surrounding communities has inspired several decades of research, both across the northern forest and at other mid- and high-latitude ecosystems around the globe. Despite these efforts, we lack a synthetic understanding of how winter climate change may impact hydrological and biogeochemical processes and the social and economic activities they support. Here, we take advantage of 100 years of meteorological observations across the northern forest region of the northeastern United States and eastern Canada to develop a suite of indicators that enable a cross-cutting understanding of (1) how winter temperatures and snow cover have been changing and (2) how these shifts may impact both ecosystems and surrounding human communities. We show that cold and snow-covered conditions have generally decreased over the past 100 years. These trends suggest positive outcomes for tree health as related to reduced fine root mortality and nutrient loss associated with winter frost but negative outcomes as related to the northward advancement and proliferation of forest insect pests. In addition to effects on vegetation, reductions in cold temperatures and snow cover are likely to have negative impacts on the ecology of the northern forest through impacts on water, soils, and wildlife. The overall loss of coldness and snow cover may also have negative consequences for logging and forest products, vector-borne diseases, and human health, recreation, and tourism, and cultural practices, which together represent important social and economic dimensions for the northern forest region. These findings advance our understanding of how our changing winters may transform the socioecological system of a region that has been defined by the contrasting rhythm of the seasons. Our research also identifies a trajectory of change that informs our expectations for the future as the climate continues to warm.

Appendix B

Text of the Green New Deal submitted to Congress.
https://www.congress.gov/bill/116th-congress/house-resolution/109/text

Text of the new Green Deal resolution submitted to Congress
Text: H.Res.109 — 116th Congress (2019-2020) All Information (Except Text)

There is one version of the bill.
Text available as:XML/HTMLXML/HTML (new window) TXTPDF (PDF provides a complete and accurate display of this text.) Tip?
Shown Here:
Introduced in House (02/07/2019)

116th CONGRESS
1st Session
H. RES. 109

Recognizing the duty of the Federal Government to create a Green New Deal.

IN THE HOUSE OF REPRESENTATIVES
February 7, 2019
Ms. Ocasio-Cortez (for herself, Mr. Hastings, Ms. Tlaib, Mr. Serrano, Mrs. Carolyn B. Maloney of New York, Mr. Vargas, Mr. Espaillat, Mr. Lynch, Ms. Velázquez, Mr. Blumenauer, Mr. Brendan F. Boyle of Pennsylvania, Mr. Castro of Texas,

Ms. Clarke of New York, Ms. Jayapal, Mr. Khanna, Mr. Ted Lieu of California, Ms. Pressley, Mr. Welch, Mr. Engel, Mr. Neguse, Mr. Nadler, Mr. McGovern, Mr. Pocan, Mr. Takano, Ms. Norton, Mr. Raskin, Mr. Connolly, Mr. Lowenthal, Ms. Matsui, Mr. Thompson of California, Mr. Levin of California, Ms. Pingree, Mr. Quigley, Mr. Huffman, Mrs. Watson Coleman, Mr. García of Illinois, Mr. Higgins of New York, Ms. Haaland, Ms. Meng, Mr. Carbajal, Mr. Cicilline, Mr. Cohen, Ms. Clark of Massachusetts, Ms. Judy Chu of California, Ms. Mucarsel-Powell, Mr. Moulton, Mr. Grijalva, Mr. Meeks, Mr. Sablan, Ms. Lee of California, Ms. Bonamici, Mr. Sean Patrick Maloney of New York, Ms. Schakowsky, Ms. DeLauro, Mr. Levin of Michigan, Ms. McCollum, Mr. DeSaulnier, Mr. Courtney, Mr. Larson of Connecticut, Ms. Escobar, Mr. Schiff, Mr. Keating, Mr. DeFazio, Ms. Eshoo, Mrs. Trahan, Mr. Gomez, Mr. Kennedy, and Ms. Waters) submitted the following resolution; which was referred to the Committee on Energy and Commerce, and in addition to the Committees on Science, Space, and Technology, Education and Labor, Transportation and Infrastructure, Agriculture, Natural Resources, Foreign Affairs, Financial Services, the Judiciary, Ways and Means, and Oversight and Reform, for a period to be subsequently determined by the Speaker, in each case for consideration of such provisions as fall within the jurisdiction of the committee concerned

RESOLUTION

Recognizing the duty of the Federal Government to create a Green New Deal.

Whereas the October 2018 report entitled "Special Report

on Global Warming of 1.5 ºC" by the Intergovernmental Panel on Climate Change and the November 2018 Fourth National Climate Assessment report found that—

(1) human activity is the dominant cause of observed climate change over the past century;

(2) a changing climate is causing sea levels to rise and an increase in wildfires, severe storms, droughts, and other extreme weather events that threaten human life, healthy communities, and critical infrastructure;

(3) global warming at or above 2 degrees Celsius beyond preindustrialized levels will cause—

(A) mass migration from the regions most affected by climate change;

(B) more than $500,000,000,000 in lost annual economic output in the United States by the year 2100;

(C) wildfires that, by 2050, will annually burn at least twice as much forest area in the western United States than was typically burned by wildfires in the years preceding 2019;

(D) a loss of more than 99 percent of all coral reefs on Earth;

(E) more than 350,000,000 more people to be exposed globally to deadly heat stress by 2050; and

(F) a risk of damage to $1,000,000,000,000 of public infrastructure and coastal real estate in the United States; and

(4) global temperatures must be kept below 1.5 degrees Celsius above preindustrialized levels to avoid the most severe impacts of a changing climate, which will require—

(A) global reductions in greenhouse gas emissions from human sources of 40 to 60 percent from 2010 levels by 2030; and

(B) net-zero global emissions by 2050;

Whereas, because the United States has historically been responsible for a disproportionate amount of greenhouse gas emissions, having emitted 20 percent of global greenhouse gas emissions through 2014, and has a high technological capacity, the United States must take a leading role in reducing emissions through economic transformation;

Whereas the United States is currently experiencing several related crises, with—

(1) life expectancy declining while basic needs, such as clean air, clean water, healthy food, and adequate health care, housing, transportation, and education, are inaccessible to a significant portion of the United States population;

(2) a 4-decade trend of wage stagnation, deindustrialization, and antilabor policies that has led to—

(A) hourly wages overall stagnating since the 1970s despite increased worker productivity;

(B) the third-worst level of socioeconomic mobility in the developed world before the Great Recession;

(C) the erosion of the earning and bargaining power of workers in the United States; and

(D) inadequate resources for public sector workers to confront the challenges of climate change at local, State, and Federal levels; and

(3) the greatest income inequality since the 1920s, with—

(A) the top 1 percent of earners accruing 91 percent of gains in the first few years of economic recovery after the Great Recession;

(B) a large racial wealth divide amounting to a difference of 20 times more wealth between the average white family and the average black family; and

(C) a gender earnings gap that results in women earning approximately 80 percent as much as men, at the median;

Whereas climate change, pollution, and environmental destruction have exacerbated systemic racial, regional, social, environmental, and economic injustices (referred to in this preamble as "systemic injustices") by disproportionately affecting indigenous peoples, communities of color, migrant communities, deindustrialized communities, depopulated rural communities, the poor, low-income workers, women, the elderly, the unhoused, people with disabilities, and youth (referred to in this preamble as "frontline and vulnerable communities");

Whereas, climate change constitutes a direct threat to the national security of the United States—

(1) by impacting the economic, environmental, and social stability of countries and communities around the world; and

(2) by acting as a threat multiplier;

Whereas the Federal Government-led mobilizations during World War II and the New Deal created the greatest middle class that the United States has ever seen, but many members of frontline and vulnerable communities were excluded from many of the economic and societal benefits of those mobilizations; and

Whereas the House of Representatives recognizes that a new national, social, industrial, and economic mobilization on a scale not seen since World War II and the New Deal era is a historic opportunity—

(1) to create millions of good, high-wage jobs in the United States;

(2) to provide unprecedented levels of prosperity and economic security for all people of the United States; and

(3) to counteract systemic injustices: Now, therefore, be it Resolved, that it is the sense of the House of Representatives that—

(1) it is the duty of the Federal Government to create a Green New Deal—

(A) to achieve net-zero greenhouse gas emissions through a fair and just transition for all communities and workers;

(B) to create millions of good, high-wage jobs and ensure prosperity and economic security for all people of the United States;

(C) to invest in the infrastructure and industry of the United States to sustainably meet the challenges of the 21st century;

(D) to secure for all people of the United States for generations to come—

(i) clean air and water;

(ii) climate and community resiliency;

(iii) healthy food;

(iv) access to nature; and

(v) a sustainable environment; and

(E) to promote justice and equity by stopping current, preventing future, and repairing historic oppression of indigenous peoples, communities of color, migrant communities, deindustrialized communities, depopulated rural communities, the poor, low-income workers, women, the elderly, the unhoused, people with disabilities, and youth (referred to in this resolution as "frontline and vulnerable communities");

(2) the goals described in subparagraphs (A) through (E) of paragraph (1) (referred to in this resolution as the "Green New Deal goals") should be accomplished through a 10-

year national mobilization (referred to in this resolution as the "Green New Deal mobilization") that will require the following goals and projects—

(A) building resiliency against climate change-related disasters, such as extreme weather, including by leveraging funding and providing investments for community-defined projects and strategies;

(B) repairing and upgrading the infrastructure in the United States, including—

(i) by eliminating pollution and greenhouse gas emissions as much as technologically feasible;

(ii) by guaranteeing universal access to clean water;

(iii) by reducing the risks posed by climate impacts; and

(iv) by ensuring that any infrastructure bill considered by Congress addresses climate change;

(C) meeting 100 percent of the power demand in the United States through clean, renewable, and zero-emission energy sources, including—

(i) by dramatically expanding and upgrading renewable power sources; and

(ii) by deploying new capacity;

(D) building or upgrading to energy-efficient, distributed, and "smart" power grids, and ensuring affordable access to electricity;

(E) upgrading all existing buildings in the United States and building new buildings to achieve maximum energy efficiency, water efficiency, safety, affordability, comfort, and durability, including through electrification;

(F) spurring massive growth in clean manufacturing in the United States and removing pollution and greenhouse gas emissions from manufacturing and industry as much as is technologically feasible, including by expanding renewable energy manufacturing and investing in existing manufacturing and industry;

(G) working collaboratively with farmers and ranchers in the United States to remove pollution and greenhouse gas emissions from the agricultural sector as much as is technologically feasible, including—

(i) by supporting family farming;

(ii) by investing in sustainable farming and land use practices that increase soil health; and

(iii) by building a more sustainable food system that ensures universal access to healthy food;

(H) overhauling transportation systems in the United States to remove pollution and greenhouse gas emissions from the transportation sector as much as is technologically feasible, including through investment in—

(i) zero-emission vehicle infrastructure and manufacturing;

(ii) clean, affordable, and accessible public transit; and

(iii) high-speed rail;

(I) mitigating and managing the long-term adverse health, economic, and other effects of pollution and climate change, including by providing funding for community-defined projects and strategies;

(J) removing greenhouse gases from the atmosphere and reducing pollution by restoring natural ecosystems through proven low-tech solutions that increase soil carbon storage, such as land preservation and afforestation;

(K) restoring and protecting threatened, endangered, and fragile ecosystems through locally appropriate and science-based projects that enhance biodiversity and support climate resiliency;

(L) cleaning up existing hazardous waste and abandoned sites, ensuring economic development and sustainability on those sites;

(M) identifying other emission and pollution sources and creating solutions to remove them; and

(N) promoting the international exchange of technology, expertise, products, funding, and services, with the aim of making the United States the international leader on climate action, and to help other countries achieve a Green New Deal;

(3) a Green New Deal must be developed through transparent and inclusive consultation, collaboration, and partnership with frontline and vulnerable communities, labor unions, worker cooperatives, civil society groups, academia, and businesses; and

(4) to achieve the Green New Deal goals and mobilization, a Green New Deal will require the following goals and projects—

(A) providing and leveraging, in a way that ensures that the public receives appropriate ownership stakes and returns on investment, adequate capital (including through community grants, public banks, and other public financing), technical expertise, supporting policies, and other forms of assistance to communities, organizations, Federal, State, and local government agencies, and businesses working on the Green New Deal mobilization;

(B) ensuring that the Federal Government takes into account the complete environmental and social costs and impacts of emissions through—

(i) existing laws;

(ii) new policies and programs; and

(iii) ensuring that frontline and vulnerable communities shall not be adversely affected;

(C) providing resources, training, and high-quality education, including higher education, to all people of the United States, with a focus on frontline and vulnerable communities, so that all people of the United States may be full and equal participants in the Green New Deal mobilization;

(D) making public investments in the research and development of new clean and renewable energy technologies and industries;

(E) directing investments to spur economic development, deepen and diversify industry and business in local and regional economies, and build wealth and community ownership, while prioritizing high-quality job creation and economic, social, and environmental benefits in frontline and vulnerable communities, and deindustrialized communities, that may otherwise struggle with the transition away from greenhouse gas intensive industries;

(F) ensuring the use of democratic and participatory processes that are inclusive of and led by frontline and vulnerable communities and workers to plan, implement, and administer the Green New Deal mobilization at the local level;

(G) ensuring that the Green New Deal mobilization creates high-quality union jobs that pay prevailing wages, hires local workers, offers training and advancement opportunities, and guarantees wage and benefit parity for workers affected by the transition;

(H) guaranteeing a job with a family-sustaining wage, adequate family and medical leave, paid vacations, and retirement security to all people of the United States;

(I) strengthening and protecting the right of all workers to organize, unionize, and collectively bargain free of coercion, intimidation, and harassment;

(J) strengthening and enforcing labor, workplace health and safety, antidiscrimination, and wage and hour standards across all employers, industries, and sectors;

(K) enacting and enforcing trade rules, procurement standards, and border adjustments with strong labor and environmental protections—

(i) to stop the transfer of jobs and pollution overseas; and

(ii) to grow domestic manufacturing in the United States;

(L) ensuring that public lands, waters, and oceans are protected, and that eminent domain is not abused;

(M) obtaining the free, prior, and informed consent of indigenous peoples for all decisions that affect indigenous peoples and their traditional territories, honoring all treaties and agreements with indigenous peoples, and protecting and enforcing the sovereignty and land rights of indigenous peoples;

(N) ensuring a commercial environment where every businessperson is free from unfair competition and domination by domestic or international monopolies; and

(O) providing all people of the United States with—

(i) high-quality health care;

(ii) affordable, safe, and adequate housing;

(iii) economic security; and

(iv) clean water, clean air, healthy and affordable food, and access to nature.

Appendix C

Charitable giving

Like many people , I am a firm believer that certain behavior can be formed or modified by where consumers or charitable benefactors put their money. Lisa M. Grasso, an environmental activist and writer recently wrote an opinion piece on how charitable giving can help improve our environment. She goes on to suggest that you can help shape the views of your own budding environmentalists. Her column appears below:

Every year I always try to find the appropriate holiday gifts. Most of the time, I get things done well in advance but many times there are the few last-minute additions to my list.

One of my favorite approaches to gift giving is to do an honorary donation or a symbolic adoption in the name of someone on my list. This is usually well received, especially with children; we discuss what we want to do and how it helps. I ask them what they care about; animals, the ocean, national parks, and other matters. This provides opportunity for discussion with kids about whatever causes you and they wish to target. I try to keep the discussion positive and age appropriate.

Once they decide who or what they want to help, I make the donation or adoption contribution in their names. Many of the organizations involved will send a card, a certificate, pictures of who or what the the target of the contribution maybe and details on how their contribution helps. Wildlife is one of our favorite focuses, and if this interests you and your little ones, read on.

Look at organizations like The World Wildlife Fund https://gifts.worldwildlife.org/gift-center/ that has global reach or National Wildlife Federation https://nwf.org with focus on North American wildlife. Among the worthwhile local organizations is the Massachusetts Audubon Society, https://www.massaudubon.org. This organization helps preserver bird habitats in my home state.

Through sites such as these, you can purchase a symbolic adoption of wide range of animals. Depending on what level you choose your kit will vary. You could get something as simple as a poster and a certificate of adoption for the older kids, or you could get the aforementioned items as well as plush animals for those that are younger! If you are shopping for younger kids, this is an awesome idea. Many kids usually have some sort of affinity for an animal out there, be it one of the many kinds of wild cats or bears, wolves, all the cool birds of prey, marine life, or something more emotive like bunnies or butterflies.

What do organizations do with the money you give them? One example of what the National Wildlife Federation does is to work on wildlife corridors. If you are familiar with the Los Angeles area it may interest you that the NWF is working with local and state authorities to create the Liberty Canyon Wildlife Crossing located near Highway 101. It will provide safe passage for Southern California's mountain lions. The NWF states that once completed it will be the largest wildlife crossing in the world, and a model for urban wildlife conservation. https://savelacougars.org/

If you and your family are concerned about protecting other wildlife or even endangered plants, and you are looking for a different and meaningful gift for someone in your life, do a search on symbolic adoptions and see if there is an organization that interests you.

If there are other causes you and the little ones feel are important, there are other symbolic gifts that can be made for people in need too. Organizations that preserve parks or build recreational trails also can use a hand. https://www.railstotrails.org/about/

Gifts like these teach the young folks in our lives to think about others and the importance of lending a hand. And from my experience, the kids like knowing they can do something to help others. Which I think many of us feel is the true spirit of the season.

As with any gift – the sooner you get it the better, but this approach also makes a great last-minute gift idea.

One more thing, check with parents to make sure they are okay with the child's name being used and with the mission of the chosen organization.

Enjoy the holiday season!

Appendix D

Recycling your old Tech

This appeared as a post on the website sustainablysimplelife. com. Some of the links cited may have been changed but a quick search on Google should find what you need.

Safe disposal of old tech

Note- please read the SERIOUS WARNING at the end of this article.

Andy is an inspiration.

Every time we talk I learn something. During a discussion, probably discussing economics, one morning she recommended a book, *The Ecology of Commerce* by Paul Hawken. I didn't agree with everything in that book but there was a premise with which I do agree and that is we do not factor in the total cost of a product. We do not realize the cost of safely disposing of a product once it is obsolete is not paid for by the manufacturer, seller, or consumer. It is often paid for by the community or the world. There may not be a direct financial outlay but we will all pay through detrimental effects. It could be as simple as a blight on the landscape or dangerous as the leeching of carcinogens into the environment.

Until the mid-20th century this wasn't much of a problem. When people did buy pre-made goods like kitchen items, appliances, or clothes they used then until they disintegrated or were handed down to another family member. Old clothes often became quilts. Many used appliances were made of metal that, if broken and not repairable, could be easily reused as scrap metal. Even most bottles brought into the home were returned for reuse.

After World War II the pace of everything seemed to increase. Car models changed dramatically every couple of years. TVs increased in size and features, and other appliances were replaced by newer and better models. More and more items that were once made of metal and wood were now made from plastic. This problem has only increased more into the 21st century. Whereas a couple married in the 1950s may have had the same telephone until the break-up of AT&T in the 1980s. There were few reasons to "upgrade".

In the past twenty years we have been upgrading products annually even though they still have useful life. We did this because something perceived as better came along. For a while it was easy to pass a computer, cell phone or flat screen TV on to someone else. But now – everyone seems to have one. Schools and other one time consumers of cast off tech refused to accept all the used products. The result is a closet full of old tech or worse – landfills filling with plastic and glass that will be there for centuries.

In the past few years a number of tech companies, retailers, and other manufacturers have realized they are part of the problem and started offering solutions. Many companies are now accepting unwanted products they once sold or manufactured.

To take advantage of these programs do a little research before buying. If you need a replacement computer, phone, or even kitchen appliance go to the manufacturers web site and see if they offer to take returns. Many of them will provide a printable pre-paid mailing label. All you have to do is provide the box. Some may offer credit toward a new purchase – or in the case of Apple an iTunes gift card. You might be surprised at what your old device is worth. Even if they don't offer anything in return at least you've kept one more item out of a landfill.

In the interest of disclosure – I do have an interest in some of the companies I mention. So you can take that into account before you make a decision.

So how do you make a decision? Well I did a little research. The list below is by no means comprehensive. I just created it to illustrate a few possibilities.

Tech -

Apple https://www.apple.com/shop/trade-in
Offers trade in of old equipment. For recent generations of computers, tablets, phones, and watches credit is available.

Samsung https://www.samsung.com/us/aboutsamsung/sustainability/environment/responsible-recycling/

More limited. They will help you find a recycler in your area or offer a mail-in option if nothing else is available.

Hewlett-Packard http://www8.hp.com/us/en/hp-information/environment/product-recycling.html

Accepts

HP has one of the most comprehensive programs for recycling devices and parts, such as laser cartridges. They might be able to help your business, too.

Dell http://www.dell.com/learn/us/en/uscorp1/dell-environment-recycling

Dell is similar to HP when it comes to return and recycling options. Dell has both commercial and consumer options.

Retail

Staples
https://www.staples.com/sbd/cre/marketing/sustainability-center/recycling-services/

Staples will accept, for recycling, products that they didn't even sell, within reasonable limits. Credit is offered in some cases. Please call your local store before showing up with a Laser printer from 1986.

Best Buy

https://www.bestbuy.com/site/clp/recycling/pcmcat149900050025.c?id=pcmcat149900050025

Like Staples, Best Buy will accept returns on many items even if they weren't purchased there. If you are returning televisions and free standing computer monitors you should call the local store for their policies.

Amazon

https://www.amazon.com/gp/help/customer/display.html?nodeId=200197550

Amazon, which straddle the retail and tech worlds, offers a number of options. You can return your Amazon labels devices (Kindle, Fire, etc) and in some cases get Amazon credit.   For non-Amazon products sold by Amazon you have the option of reselling them on Amazon, a sort of consignment options

A Surprise

Hasbro

https://csr2.hasbro.com/en-us

Anyone with kids will tell you they have a lot of useless broken parts of toys lying around or stuffed into boxes. Hasbro is the first toy manufacturer to accept their products (only their products). Return shipping is free but there is no provision for credit. The returned items will be recycled. Mostly into playground equipment.

Serious warning before returning any tech products or any product that may store information.

Before you return any tech product that may have data, photos, emails, logins, or passwords, etc stored check the following. DO THIS EVEN IF YOU ARE TRADING IN TO THE SAME MANUFACTURER

Start the device:

Remove or deactivate from streaming services, email settings and social media apps.

Reset to factory default

Remove any media. This includes USB drives, media cards, DVDs, CDs, and need I say, floppy disks. If it's that old.

For old laptops and desktop computers you can download software that will wipe all data off of internals drives.

If you can't reboot the old device contact a technical support professional and ask what can be done.

With only a little effort you save just that much more plastic and potentially toxic materials from a landfill.

ACKNOWLEDGEMENTS

As you may have noticed, this book was meant to convey facts as I have researched them and a lot of my personal opinions.

For the research, I would like to acknowledge the work of the researchers, writers, and organization – both public and private cited. Much of the information is readily available through the respective organizations' websites or in articles and books at your local public library. So, anyone who disagrees with me has access to the same information.

For my opinions, I suppose I have to thank everyone who has every engaged me in debate, be it family, friends, teachers, or colleagues. My parents never discouraged expressing my opinions but also reminded me to respect the opinions of others. Even if I didn't like them.

Family events, with my siblings and their spouses, always seem to involve one spirited discussion or another, be it politics or sports. I have seven siblings so by spirited, I mean there's three or four debates going on at one time. Sometimes in more than one language.

Many of my professors at Bridgewater State College, who were instrumental in encouraging my natural skepticism while keeping a lid on cynicism.

There are the contributions of my self-described liberal friend, Lisa. Our conversations over coffee or lunch usually center around topics such as family, football, music, television, economics or the environment. The conversations have ended with agreements on football or music. The other topics often end up with agreements on goals but disagreements over the ways to meet them. Either way, lunch always ends with an agreement to 'do this again'. Lisa has made several direct contributions to this book.

Most importantly, I have to the contributions of my lovely wife of many years, Louise. Without her encouragement, feedback, and support I wouldn't have gotten past the first chapter.

Louise always seems to know what I am capable before I do. With her encouragement, I have been able to finish graduate school while working full-time, participate several times in a grueling athletic charitable fund-raising event, write several works of fiction (in the editing process), and this book. All these years she has patiently listened to me as I get on my soapbox and rant about one issue or another – be it politics or who was the best actor to play James Bond. She does not hesitate to tell me if I am wrong. Louise is also a talented graphic designer and has created the cover design for both print and electronic editions of this book.

Without my wife, friends and family this book would not have been written.

Sources:

We live in age that is an amateur researcher's dream. As I mentioned in the section of doing your own research, the problem is getting information that is useful and reliable, not just something that agrees with your point of view. Most of what I have researched has been footnoted for the convenience of the reader. In the future I hope to add to this book but will always check previous citations to be certain they are still available.

RAC
North Attleborough, Massachusetts

www.ingramcontent.com/pod-product-compliance
Lightning Source LLC
Chambersburg PA
CBHW070658250726
48662CB00001B/179